THE VEGETARIAN
Gourmet

THE VEGETARIAN Gourmet

ACROPOLIS BOOKS

First published in 1995 by Ultimate Editions

© Anness Publishing Limited 1995

Ultimate Editions is an imprint of
Anness Publishing Limited
1 Boundary Row
London SE1 8HP

This edition distributed in Canada by
Book Express, an imprint of
Raincoast Book Distribution Limited

Distributed in Australia by Reed Editions

ISBN 1 86035 035 6

Previously published as part of a larger compendium,
The Ultimate Vegetarian Cookbook

Editorial Director: Joanna Lorenz
Project Editor: Samantha Gray
Designer: Adrian Morris
Photographer: Michael Michaels
Home Economist: Wendy Lee

Typeset by MC Typeset Limited
Printed and bound in Singapore

 THE LEAF SYMBOL NEXT TO A RECIPE INDICATES THAT IT IS SUITABLE FOR VEGANS.

MEASUREMENTS
Three sets of equivalent measurements have been provided in the recipes here, in the following order:
Metric, Imperial and American.
It is essential that units of measurement are not mixed within each recipe.
Where conversions result in awkward numbers, these have been rounded for convenience,
but are accurate enough to produce successful results.

CONTENTS

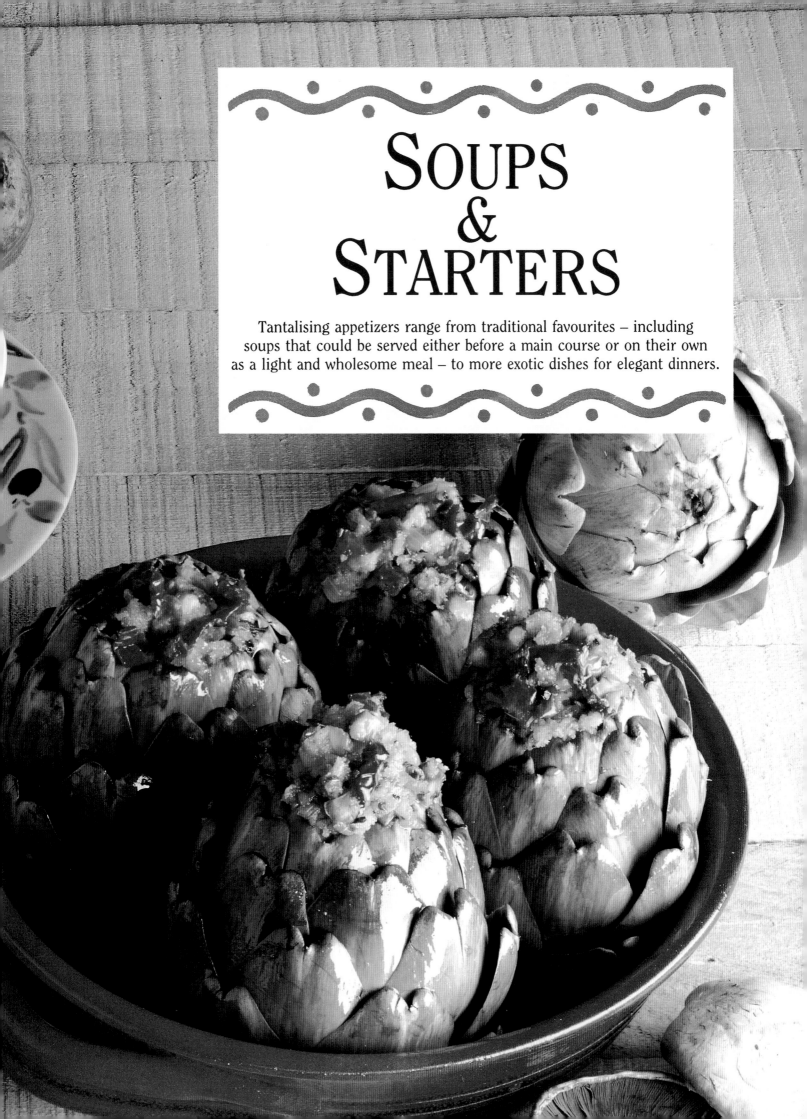

SOUPS & STARTERS

Tantalising appetizers range from traditional favourites – including soups that could be served either before a main course or on their own as a light and wholesome meal – to more exotic dishes for elegant dinners.

Egg Flower Soup

For the very best flavour, you do need to use a homemade stock for this soup. The egg sets into pretty strands giving the soup a flowery look, hence the name.

SERVES 6
1 litre/1¾ pints/4 cups stock
45 ml/3 tbsp light soy sauce
30 ml/2 tbsp dry sherry or vermouth
3 spring onions, diagonally sliced
small piece fresh root ginger, shredded
4 large lettuce leaves, shredded
5 ml/1 tsp sesame seed oil
2 eggs, beaten
salt and ground black pepper
sesame seeds, to garnish

1 Pour the stock into a large saucepan. Add all the ingredients except the eggs and seeds. Bring to the boil and then cook for about 2 minutes.

2 Very carefully, pour the eggs in a thin, steady stream into the centre of the boiling liquid.

3 Count to three then quickly stir the soup. The egg will begin to cook and form long threads. Season to taste, ladle the soup into warm bowls and serve immediately sprinkled with sesame seeds.

Broccoli and Blue Brie Soup

A popular vegetable, broccoli makes a delicious soup with an appetizing deep green colour. For a tasty tang, stir in some cubes of blue Brie cheese just before serving.

SERVES 6
1 onion, chopped
450 g/1 lb broccoli spears, chopped
1 large courgette, chopped
1 large carrot, chopped
1 medium potato, chopped
25 g/1 oz/2 tbsp butter
30 ml/2 tbsp sunflower oil
2 litres/3½ pints/8 cups stock or water
about 75 g/3 oz blue Brie (or Dolcellate) cheese, cubed
salt and ground black pepper
almond flakes, to garnish (optional)

VARIATION

Try using cauliflower instead of broccoli in this recipe. Stilton is a tasty alternative to Brie.

1 Put all the vegetables into a large saucepan, together with the butter and oil plus about 45 ml/3 tbsp stock or water.

2 Heat the ingredients until sizzling and stir well. Cover and cook gently for 15 minutes, shaking the pan occasionally, until all the vegetables soften.

3 Add the rest of the stock or water, season and bring to a boil, then cover and simmer gently for about 25–30 minutes.

4 Strain the vegetables and reserve the liquid. Purée the vegetables in a food processor or blender then return them to the pan with the reserved liquid.

5 Bring the soup back to a gentle boil and stir in the cheese until it melts. (Don't let the soup boil too hard or the cheese will become stringy.) Season to taste and garnish with a scattering of almond flakes.

Borscht

A simply stunning colour, this classic Russian soup is ideal to serve when you want to make something a little different. The flavour matures and improves too if it is made the day before it is needed.

SERVES 6
1 onion, chopped
450 g/1 lb raw beetroot, peeled and chopped
1 large cooking apple, chopped
2 celery sticks, chopped
½ red pepper, chopped
115 g/4 oz mushrooms, chopped
25 g/1 oz/2 tbsp butter
30 ml/2 tbsp sunflower oil
2 litres/3½ pints/8 cups stock or water
5 ml/1 tsp cumin seeds
pinch dried thyme
1 large bay leaf
fresh lemon juice
salt and ground black pepper
150 ml/¼ pint/⅔ cup soured cream
few sprigs fresh dill, to garnish

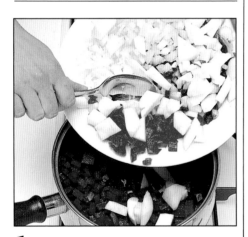

1 Place all the chopped vegetables into a large saucepan with the butter, oil and 45 ml/3 tbsp of the stock or water. Cover and cook gently for about 15 minutes, shaking the pan occasionally.

2 Stir in the cumin seeds and cook for a minute, then add the remaining stock or water, dried thyme, bay leaf, lemon juice and seasoning.

3 Bring to the boil, then cover and turn down to a gentle simmer. Cook for about 30 minutes.

4 Strain the vegetables and reserve the liquid. Pass the vegetables through a food processor or blender until they are smooth and creamy.

5 Return the vegetables to the pan, stir in the reserved stock and reheat. Check the seasoning.

6 Serve the borscht with swirls of soured cream and topped with a few sprigs of fresh dill.

VARIATION

This soup can be served fairly thick, as long as the vegetables are finely chopped first.

Beetroot is something of an under-valued vegetable, although popular in many European countries. For example, it is delicious served as a hot vegetable accompaniment with a creamy bechamel sauce and topped with crisp breadcrumbs. Alternatively, try it raw and coarsely grated, then tossed in dressing for a side salad.

Garlicky Mushrooms

Serve these on toast for a quick, tasty starter or pop them into small ramekins and serve with slices of warm crusty bread. Use some shitake mushrooms, if you can find them, for a richer flavour.

SERVES 4
450 g/1 lb button mushrooms, sliced
   if large
45 ml/3 tbsp olive oil
45 ml/3 tbsp stock or water
30 ml/2 tbsp dry sherry (optional)
3 garlic cloves, crushed
115 g/4 oz low fat soft cheese
30 ml/2 tbsp fresh parsley, chopped
15 ml/1 tbsp fresh chives, chopped
salt and ground black pepper

1 Put the mushrooms into a large saucepan with the olive oil, stock or water and sherry, if using. Heat until bubbling then cover and simmer for 5 minutes.

2 Add the garlic and stir well. Cook for a further 2 minutes. Remove the mushrooms with a slotted spoon and set them aside. Cook the liquor until it reduces down to 30 ml/2 tbsp. Remove from the heat and stir in the cheese and herbs.

3 Stir the mixture well until the cheese melts then return the mushrooms to the pan so that they become coated with the cheesy mixture. Season to taste.

4 Pile the mushrooms onto thick slabs of hot toast. Alternatively, spoon them into four ramekins and serve accompanied by slices of crusty bread.

Ricotta and Borlotti Bean Pâté

A lovely light yet full-flavoured pâté. For an attractive presentation, spoon the pâté into small, oiled ring moulds, turn out and fill with some whole borlotti beans, simply dressed with lemon juice, olive oil and fresh herbs.

SERVES 4
1 × 400 g/14 oz can borlotti beans,
   drained
1 garlic clove, crushed
175 g/6 oz ricotta cheese (or other cream
   cheese)
50 g/2 oz/4 tbsp butter, melted
juice of ½ lemon
salt and ground black pepper
30 ml/2 tbsp fresh parsley, chopped
15 ml/1 tbsp fresh thyme or dill, chopped
TO SERVE
extra canned beans (optional)
fresh lemon juice, olive oil and chopped
   herbs (optional)
salad leaves, radish slices and few sprigs
   fresh dill, to garnish

1 Blend the beans, garlic, cheese, butter, lemon juice and seasoning in a food processor until smooth.

2 Add the chopped herbs and continue to blend. Spoon into one serving dish or four lightly oiled ramekins, the bases lined with discs of non-stick baking paper. Chill the pâté so that it sets firm.

3 If serving with extra beans, dress them with lemon juice, olive oil and herbs, season well and spoon on top. Garnish with salad leaves and serve with warm crusty bread or toast.

4 If serving individually, turn each pâté out of its ramekin onto a small plate and remove the disc of paper. Top with radish slices and sprigs of dill.

VARIATION

You could try other canned pulses for this recipe, although the softer lentils would not be suitable. Butter (lima) beans are surprisingly good. For an attractive presentation fill the centre with dark red kidney beans and chopped fresh green beans.

Twice-baked Goats' Cheese Soufflés

A good chef's trick is to reheat small baked soufflés out of their ramekins to serve with a salad. They puff up again and the outsides become nice and crispy. If you prefer, you can substitute another full-flavoured cheese such as Cheddar or Parmesan.

SERVES 6
25 g/1 oz/2 tbsp butter
25 g/1 oz/3 tbsp plain flour
300 ml/½ pint/1¼ cups hot milk
pinch cayenne pepper
squeeze of lemon juice
salt and ground black pepper
100 g/3½ oz semi-hard goats' cheese, crumbled
2 eggs, separated
melted butter, for brushing
25 g/1 oz/3 tbsp dried breadcrumbs
25 g/1 oz/3 tbsp ground hazelnuts or walnuts
2 egg whites
salad garnish (optional)

1 Melt the butter and stir in the flour. Cook to a roux for a minute then gradually whisk in the hot milk to make a thick white sauce.

VARIATION

There is another good chef's trick – making soufflés in advance and chilling them unbaked. It helps to add an extra egg white or two when whisking, depending on the mixture. It is also possible to freeze unbaked soufflés in small ramekins and then to bake them from frozen, allowing an extra 5 or 10 minutes' baking time.

2 Simmer for a minute then season with cayenne, lemon juice, salt and pepper. Remove the pan from the heat and stir in the cheese until it melts. Cool slightly then beat in the egg yolks.

3 Brush the insides of six ramekins with the melted butter and coat them with the breadcrumbs and nuts mixed together. Shake out any excess.

4 Preheat the oven to 190°C/375°F/ Gas 5 and prepare a bain marie – a roasting pan with boiling water.

5 Whisk the four egg whites to the soft peak stage and carefully fold them into the main mixture using a figure of eight motion. Spoon into the ramekins.

6 Place the soufflés in the bain marie and bake for about 12–15 minutes until risen and golden brown. You can of course serve them at this stage; otherwise allow to cool then chill.

7 To serve twice-baked, reheat the oven to the same temperature. Run a knife round the inside of each ramekin and turn out each soufflé onto a baking tray.

8 Bake the soufflés for about 12 minutes. Serve on prepared plates with a dressed salad garnish.

Stuffed Artichokes 🌿

Globe artichokes are a little fiddly to prepare but their delicious taste makes it all worthwhile, especially when stuffed with nuts, mushrooms and sun-dried tomatoes. This dish can be prepared in advance and reheated before serving.

SERVES 4
4 medium globe artichokes
salt
lemon slices
STUFFING
1 medium onion, chopped
1 garlic clove, crushed
45 ml/3 tbsp olive oil
115 g/4 oz mushrooms, chopped
1 medium carrot, grated
40 g/1½ oz sun-dried tomatoes in oil, drained and sliced
leaves from a sprig of thyme
about 45–60 ml/3–4 tbsp water
ground black pepper
115 g/4 oz/2 cups fresh breadcrumbs
extra olive oil, to cook
fresh parsley, chopped, to garnish

1 Boil the artichokes in plenty of salted water with a few slices of lemon for about 30 minutes, or until a leaf pulls easily from the base. Strain through a colander and cool the artichokes, laying them upside down.

2 To make the stuffing for the artichokes, gently fry the onion and garlic in the oil for 5 minutes, then add the mushrooms, carrot, sun-dried tomatoes and thyme.

3 Stir in the water, season well and cook for a further 5 minutes, then mix in the breadcrumbs.

VARIATION

For a lighter meal, rather than stuff the artichokes, you could simply fill the centres with home-made mayonnaise or serve with a dish of vinaigrette or melted butter for dipping the leaves.

4 Pull the artichoke leaves apart and pull out the purple-tipped central leaves. Using a small teaspoon, scrape out the hairy choke, making sure that you remove it all. Discard it.

5 Spoon the stuffing into the centre of the artichoke, and push the leaves back into shape. Put the artichokes into an ovenproof dish and pour a little oil into the centre of each one.

6 Half an hour before serving, heat the oven to 190°C/375°F/Gas 5 and bake the artichokes for about 20–25 minutes until heated through. Serve garnished with a little chopped fresh parsley on top.

Bruschetta with Goats' Cheese and Tapenade

Simple to prepare in advance, this appetizing dish can be served as a starter or at finger buffets. Make sure that you finely chop the ingredients for the tapenade.

SERVES 4–6
TAPENADE
1 × 400 g/14 oz can black olives, stoned and finely chopped
50 g/2 oz sun-dried tomatoes in oil, chopped
30 ml/2 tbsp capers, chopped
15 ml/1 tbsp green peppercorns, in brine, crushed
45–60 ml/3–4 tbsp olive oil
2 garlic cloves, crushed
45 ml/3 tbsp fresh basil, chopped, or 5 ml/1 tsp dried basil
salt and ground black pepper
BASES
12 slices Ciabatta or other crusty bread
olive oil, for brushing
2 garlic cloves, halved
115 g/4 oz soft goats' cheese (or plain cream cheese)
fresh herb sprigs, to garnish

1 Mix the tapenade ingredients all together and check the seasoning. It should not need too much. Allow to marinate overnight, if possible.

2 To make the bruschetta, grill both sides of the bread lightly until golden. Brush one side with oil and then rub with a cut clove of garlic. Set aside until ready to serve.

3 Spread the bruschetta with the cheese, roughing it up with a fork, and spoon the tapenade on top. Garnish with sprigs of herbs.

COOK'S TIP

The bruschetta is nicest grilled over a open barbecue flame, if possible. Failing that a grill will do, but avoid using a toaster – it gives too even a colour and the bruschetta is supposed to look quite rustic.

Warm Avocadoes with Tangy Topping

Lightly grilled with a tasty topping of red onions and cheese, this dish makes a delightful alternative to the rather humdrum avocado vinaigrette.

SERVES 4
1 small red onion, sliced
1 garlic clove, crushed
15 ml/1 tbsp sunflower oil
Worcestershire sauce
2 ripe avocados, halved and stoned
2 small tomatoes, sliced
15 ml/1 tbsp fresh chopped basil, marjoram or parsley
50 g/2 oz Lancashire or Mozzarella cheese, sliced
salt and ground black pepper

1 Gently fry the onion and garlic in the oil for about 5 minutes until just softened. Shake in a little Worcestershire sauce.

2 Preheat a grill. Place the avocado halves on the grill pan and spoon the onions into the centre.

3 Divide the tomato slices and fresh herbs between the four halves and top each one with the cheese.

4 Season well and grill until the cheese melts and starts to brown.

VARIATION

Avocadoes are wonderful served in other hot dishes too. Try them chopped and tossed into hot pasta or sliced and layered in a lasagne.

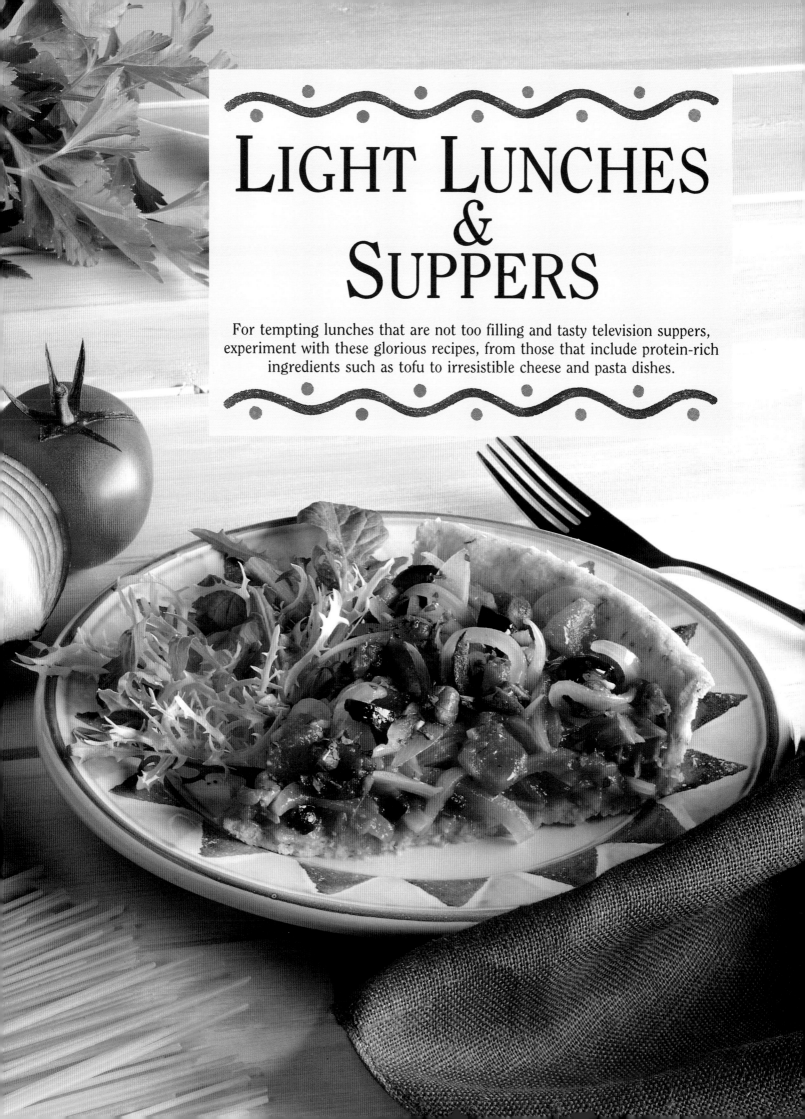

LIGHT LUNCHES
&
SUPPERS

For tempting lunches that are not too filling and tasty television suppers, experiment with these glorious recipes, from those that include protein-rich ingredients such as tofu to irresistible cheese and pasta dishes.

Mexican Brunch Eggs

Instead of eggs on toast, why not try them on fried corn tortillas with chillies and creamy avocado? Canned tortillas are readily available from larger supermarkets or delicatessens.

SERVES 4
oil, for frying
8 tortilla corn pancakes
1 avocado
1 large tomato
50 g/2 oz/4 tbsp butter
8 eggs
4 jalepeno chillies, sliced
salt and ground black pepper
15 ml/1 tbsp fresh coriander, chopped,
   to garnish

1 Heat the oil and fry the tortillas for a few seconds each side. Remove and drain. Keep the tortillas warm.

2 Halve, stone and peel the avocado, then cut into slices. Dip the tomato into boiling water, then skin and chop roughly.

3 Melt the butter in a frying pan and fry the eggs, in batches, sunny side up.

4 Place two tortillas on four plates, slip an egg on each and top with sliced chillies, avocado and tomato. Season and serve garnished with fresh coriander.

Fried Tomatoes with Polenta Crust

If you saw the film 'Fried Green Tomatoes' then you should enjoy this dish! No need to search for home-grown green tomatoes – any slightly under-ripe ones will do.

SERVES 4
4 large firm under-ripe tomatoes
115 g/4 oz/1 cup polenta or coarse
   cornmeal
5 ml//1 tsp dried oregano
2.5 ml/½ tsp garlic powder
plain flour, for dredging
1 egg, beaten with seasoning
oil, for deep fat frying

1 Cut the tomatoes into thick slices. Mix the polenta or cornmeal with the oregano and garlic powder.

2 Put the flour, egg and polenta into different bowls. Dip the tomato slices into the flour, then into the egg and finally into the polenta.

3 Fill a shallow frying pan a third full of oil and heat steadily until quite hot.

4 Slip the tomato slices into the oil carefully, a few at a time, and fry on each side until crisp. Remove and drain. Repeat with the remaining tomatoes, reheating the oil in between. Serve with salad.

Pissaladière

A French Mediterranean classic, this is a delicious and colourful tart full of punchy flavour. Ideally, put the base and fillings together just when serving so the base remains crisp.

SERVES 6

PASTRY
225 g/8 oz/2 cups plain flour
115 g/4 oz/8 tbsp butter or sunflower margarine
5 ml/1 tsp dried mixed herbs
pinch salt

FILLING
2 large onions, thinly sliced
2 garlic cloves, crushed
45 ml/3 tbsp olive oil
fresh nutmeg, grated, to taste
1 × 400 g/14 oz can chopped tomatoes
5 ml/1 tsp sugar
leaves from small sprig of thyme
salt and ground black pepper
75 g/3 oz/⅔ cup stoned black olives, sliced
30 ml/2 tbsp capers
fresh parsley, chopped, to garnish

1 Rub the flour and butter or margarine together until it forms fine crumbs, then mix in the herbs and salt. Mix to a firm dough with cold water. Preheat the oven to 190°C/375°F/Gas 5.

2 Roll out and line a 21 cm/9 in flan dish and bake blind, removing the baking beans and paper for the last 5 minutes for the pastry to crisp up. Cool.

3 Gently fry the onions and garlic in the oil for about 10 minutes until quite soft and mix in the nutmeg.

4 Stir in the tomatoes, sugar, thyme and seasoning and simmer gently for about 10 minutes until the mixture is reduced and slightly syrupy.

5 Remove from the heat and allow to cool. Mix in the olives and capers.

6 When ready to serve, spoon into the flan case, sprinkle with some fresh chopped parsley and serve at room temperature.

VARIATION

To serve Pissaladière hot, top with grated cheese and grill until the cheese is golden and bubbling. The crisp-baked pastry case can be used as a base for a number of other vegetable mixtures. Try filling it with a Russian Salad – chopped, cooked root vegetables, including potato and carrot, mixed with peas, beans and onions, blended with mayonnaise and soured cream. Top with slices of hard-boiled egg and garnish with chopped fresh herbs.

Multi Mushroom Stroganoff

A pan fry of sliced mushrooms swirled with soured cream is made especially interesting if two or three varieties of mushroom are used. It is even more delicious if you can incorporate woodland or wild mushrooms.

SERVES 3–4
45 ml/3 tbsp olive oil
450 g/1 lb edible mushrooms (including ceps, shiitakes or oysters), sliced
3 spring onions, sliced
2 garlic cloves, crushed
30 ml/2 tbsp dry sherry or vermouth
salt and ground black pepper
300 ml/½ pint/1¼ cups soured cream or crème fraîche
15 ml/1 tbsp fresh marjoram or thyme leaves, chopped
fresh parsley, chopped

1 Heat the oil in a large frying pan and fry the mushrooms gently, stirring them occasionally until they are softened and just cooked.

2 Add the spring onions, garlic and sherry or vermouth and cook for a minute more. Season well.

3 Stir in the soured cream or crème fraîche and heat to just below boiling. Stir in the marjoram or thyme then scatter over the parsley. Serve with rice, pasta or boiled new potatoes.

Butter Bean and Pesto Pasta

Buy good quality, ready-made pesto, rather than making your own. Pesto forms the basis of several very tasty sauces, and it is especially good with butter beans.

SERVES 4
225 g/8 oz pasta shapes
salt and ground black pepper
fresh nutmeg, grated
30 ml/2 tbsp extra virgin olive oil
1 × 400 g/14 oz can butter beans, drained
45 ml/3 tbsp pesto sauce
150 ml/¼ pint/⅔ cup single cream
TO SERVE
45 ml/3 tbsp pine nuts
cheese, grated (optional)
sprigs of fresh basil, to garnish (optional)

1 Boil the pasta until *al dente*, then drain, leaving it a little wet. Return the pasta to the pan, season, and stir in the nutmeg and oil.

2 Heat the beans in a saucepan with the pesto and cream, stirring it until it begins to simmer. Toss the beans and pesto into the pasta and mix well.

3 Serve in bowls topped with pine nuts, and add a little grated cheese and basil sprigs if you wish.

Eggs Benedict with Quick Hollandaise

Traditional Hollandaise sauce is tricky to make without it curdling. To make it quickly, yet still achieve a thick and creamy sauce, use a blender or food processor. Hollandaise sauce is simply delicious served over poached eggs on hot toasted muffins.

SERVES 4
2 egg yolks
5 ml/1 tsp dry mustard
good pinch each salt and ground black
   pepper
15 ml/1 tbsp wine vinegar or lemon juice
175 g/6 oz/¾ cup butter
4 muffins, split
butter or low fat spread
4 large eggs
30 ml/2 tbsp capers
a little fresh parsley, chopped, to garnish

---

1 Blend the egg yolks with the mustard and seasoning in a blender or food processor for a few seconds until well mixed. Mix in the vinegar or lemon juice.

2 Heat the butter until it is on the point of bubbling then, with the machine still running, slowly pour the butter onto the egg yolks.

3 The mixture should emulsify instantly and become thick and creamy. Switch off the blender and set the sauce aside.

4 Toast the split muffins. Cut four of the halves in two and lightly butter. Place the four uncut halves on warmed plates and leave unbuttered.

5 Poach the eggs either in gently simmering water or in an egg poacher. Drain well and slip carefully onto the muffin halves.

6 Spoon the sauce over the muffins and then sprinkle with capers and parsley. Serve immediately with the buttered muffin quarters.

VARIATION

This classic American brunch dish is said to have originated in New York, and is ideal to serve on a special occasion such as a birthday treat or New Year's day.

Instead of the toasted muffin, you could make more of a main meal by serving the dish on a bed of lightly steamed or blanched spinach mixed with quick fried sliced mushrooms and onions. The quick Hollandaise sauce is of course ideal as an all-purpose serving sauce for vegetables, baked potatoes, cauliflower and broccoli.

Quick Basmati and Nut Pilaff

Light and fragrant basmati rice from the foothills of the Himalayas cooks perfectly using this simple pilaff method. Use whatever nuts are your favourite – even unsalted peanuts are good, although almonds, cashews or pistachios are more exotic.

SERVES 4–6
225 g/8 oz/1¼ cups basmati rice
1 onion, chopped
1 garlic clove, crushed
1 large carrot, coarsely grated
15–30 ml/1–2 tbsp sunflower oil
5 ml/1 tsp cumin seeds
10 ml/2 tsp ground coriander
10 ml/2 tsp black mustard seeds (optional)
4 cardamom pods
450 ml/¾ pint/2 cups stock or water
1 bay leaf
salt and ground black pepper
75 g/3 oz/½ cup unsalted nuts
fresh chopped parsley or coriander,
  to garnish

RINSING BASMATI

For light, fluffy grains basmati rice is best rinsed before cooking to remove any surface starch. The traditional method is to put the rice into a large bowl of cold water. Swill the grains around with your hands then tip out the cloudy water. (The rice will quickly sink to the bottom.) Repeat this action about five times. Ideally, leave the rice to soak for 30 minutes in the last rinsing water. This ensures a lighter, fluffier grain.

1 Wash the rice either by the traditional Indian method (see note) or in a sieve under a running tap. If there is time, soak the rice for 30 minutes, then drain well in a sieve.

2 In a large shallow pan, gently fry the onion, garlic and carrot in the oil for a few minutes.

3 Stir in the rice and spices and cook for a further minute or two so that the grains are coated in oil.

4 Pour in the stock or water, add the bay leaf and season well. Bring to a boil, cover and simmer very gently for about 10 minutes.

5 Remove from the heat without lifting the lid – this helps the rice to firm up and cook further. Leave for about 5 minutes.

6 If the rice is cooked, there will be small steam holes in the centre. Discard the bay leaf and cardamom pods.

7 Stir in the nuts and check the seasoning. Scatter the mixture with the chopped parsley or coriander. This whole dish can be made ahead and reheated.

Spaghetti with Feta

We think of pasta as being essentially Italian but, in fact, the Greeks have a great appetite for it too and it complements beautifully the tangy, full-flavoured feta cheese.

SERVES 2–3
115 g/4 oz spaghetti
1 garlic clove
30 ml/2 tbsp extra virgin olive oil
8 cherry tomatoes, halved
a little freshly grated nutmeg
salt and ground black pepper
75 g/3 oz feta cheese, crumbled
15 ml/1 tbsp chopped fresh basil
a few black olives (optional), to serve

1 Boil the spaghetti in plenty of lightly salted water according to the instructions on the pack, then drain.

2 In the same pan gently heat the garlic clove in the oil for a minute or two then add the cherry tomatoes.

3 Increase the heat to fry the tomatoes lightly for a minute, then remove the garlic and discard.

4 Toss in the spaghetti, season with the nutmeg and seasoning to taste then stir in the crumbled feta and basil.

5 Check the seasoning, remembering that feta can be quite salty, and serve hot topped with olives if liked.

Potatoes with Blue Cheese and Walnuts

We are so used to eating potatoes as a side dish, we forget they can be a good main meal too. This dish is so versatile it can be served as either. Use Stilton, Danish blue, Blue Brie or any other blue veined cheese.

SERVES 4
450 g/1 lb small new potatoes
small head of celery, sliced
small red onion, sliced
115 g/4 oz blue cheese, mashed
150 ml/¼ pint/⅔ cup single cream
salt and ground black pepper
100 g/3½ oz/½ cup walnut pieces
30 ml/2 tbsp fresh parsley, chopped

1 Cover the potatoes with water and boil for about 15 minutes, adding the sliced celery and onion to the pan for the last 5 minutes or so.

2 Drain the vegetables and put them into a shallow serving dish.

3 In a small saucepan melt the cheese in the cream, slowly, stirring occasionally. Do not allow the mixture to boil but heat it until it scalds.

4 Season the sauce to taste. Pour it over the vegetables and scatter over the walnuts and parsley. Serve hot.

MAIN COURSES

Create healthy and satisfying meals that make the most of the wonderful variety of herbs and spices, as well as nutritious ingredients such as lentils, rice and vegetables.

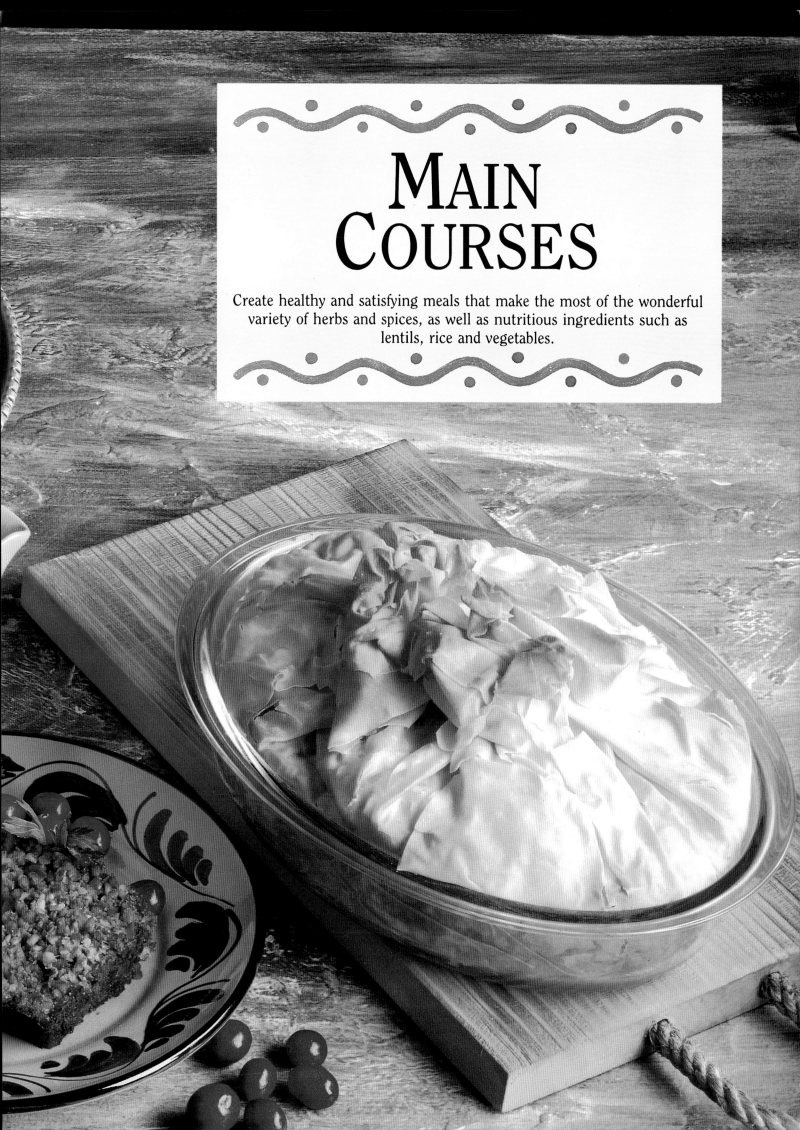

Sprouting Beans and Pak Choi

Supermarkets are fast becoming
cosmopolitan and many stock ethnic
fresh vegetables.

SERVES 4
45 ml/3 tbsp groundnut oil
3 spring onions, sliced
2 garlic cloves, cut in slivers
2.5 cm/1 in cube fresh root
ginger, cut in slivers
1 carrot, cut in thin sticks
150 g/5 oz sprouting beans (e.g. lentils,
mung beans, chick peas)
1 × 200 g/7 oz pak choi cabbage,
shredded
50 g/2 oz/½ cup unsalted cashew nuts or
halved almonds
SAUCE
45 ml/3 tbsp light soy sauce
30 ml/2 tbsp dry sherry
15 ml/1 tbsp sesame oil
150 ml/¼ pint/⅔ cup cold water
5 ml/1 tsp cornflour
5 ml/1 tsp clear honey
ground black pepper

1 Heat the oil in a large wok and stir-fry
the onions, garlic, ginger and carrot for 2
minutes. Add the sprouting beans and fry
for another 2 minutes, stirring and
tossing them together.

2 Add the pak choi and nuts or almonds
and stir-fry until the cabbage leaves are
just wilting. Quickly mix all the sauce
ingredients together in a jug and pour
them into the wok, stirring immediately.

3 The vegetables will be coated in a
thin, glossy sauce. Season and serve as
soon as possible.

Thai Tofu Curry

Thai food is a marvellous mixture of
Chinese and Indian styles, plus other
exotic ingredients.

SERVES 4
2 × 200 g/7 oz packs tofu curd, cubed
30 ml/2 tbsp light soy sauce
30 ml/2 tbsp groundnut oil
PASTE
1 small onion, chopped
2 fresh green chillies, seeded and
chopped
2 garlic cloves, chopped
15 ml/1 tbsp grated gresh gallingale or
5 ml/1 tsp grated fresh ginger
2 Thai kaffir leaves or 5 ml/1 tsp lime rind,
grated
10 ml/2 tsp coriander berries, crushed
10 ml/2 tsp cumin seeds, crushed
45 ml/3 tbsp fresh coriander, chopped
15 ml/1 tbsp Thai fish sauce (Nam pla) or
soy sauce
juice of 1 lime or small lemon
5 ml/1 tsp sugar
25 g/1 oz creamed coconut dissolved in
150 ml/¼ pint/⅔ cup boiling water
GARNISH
thin slices fresh red chilli or red pepper
fresh coriander leaves

1 Toss the tofu cubes in soy sauce and
leave to marinate for 15 minutes or so
while you prepare the paste.

2 Put all the paste ingredients into a
food processor and grind until smooth.

3 To cook, heat the oil in a wok until
quite hot. Drain the tofu cubes and stir fry
at a high temperature until well browned
on all sides and just firm. Drain on
kitchen paper towel.

4 Wipe out the wok. Pour in the paste
and stir well. Return the tofu to the wok
and mix it into the paste, reheating the
ingredients as you stir.

5 Serve this dish on a flat platter
garnished with red chilli or pepper and
chopped coriander. Bowls of Thai
fragrant or jasmine rice are the perfect
accompaniment to the curry.

Festive Jalousie

An excellent puff pastry pie to serve either on Christmas Day or at anytime during the holiday period. Chinese dried chestnuts make an excellent substitute for fresh ones when soaked and cooked. Or you could drain a can of chestnuts.

SERVES 6
450 g/1 lb puff pastry, thawed if frozen
450 g/1 lb Brussels sprouts, trimmed
about 16 whole chestnuts, peeled if fresh
1 large red pepper, sliced
1 large onion, sliced
45 ml/3 tbsp sunflower oil
1 egg yolk, beaten with 15 ml/1 tbsp
  water
SAUCE
40 g/1½ oz/scant ½ cup plain flour
40 g/1½ oz/3 tbsp butter
300 ml/½ pint/1¼ cups milk
75 g/3 oz Cheddar cheese, grated
30 ml/2 tbsp dry sherry
good pinch dried sage
salt and ground black pepper
45 ml/3 tbsp fresh parsley, chopped

2 Blanch the Brussels sprouts for 4 minutes in 300 ml/½ pint/1¼ cups boiling water then drain, reserving the water. Refresh the sprouts under cold running water.

3 Cut each chestnut in half. Lightly fry the red pepper and onion in the oil for 5 minutes. Set aside till later.

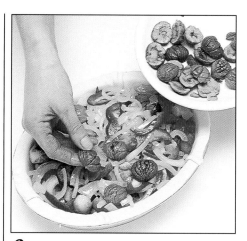

6 Fit the larger piece of pastry into your pie dish and layer the sprouts, chestnuts, peppers and onions on top. Trickle over the sauce, making sure it seeps through to wet the vegetables.

1 Roll out the pastry to make two large rectangles, roughly the size of your dish. The pastry should be about 6 mm/¼ in thick and one rectangle should be slightly larger than the other. Set the pastry aside in the refrigerator.

4 Make up the sauce by beating the flour, butter and milk together over a medium heat. Beat the sauce continuously, bringing it to the boil, stirring until it is thickened and smooth.

5 Stir in the reserved sprout water, and the cheese, sherry, sage and seasoning. Simmer for 3 minutes to reduce and mix in the parsley.

7 Brush the pastry edges with beaten egg yolk and fit the second pastry sheet on top, pressing the edges well to seal them.

8 Crimp, knock up the edges then mark the centre. Glaze well all over with egg yolk. Set aside to rest somewhere cool while you preheat the oven to 200°C/400°F/Gas 6. Bake for 30–40 minutes until golden brown and crisp.

Greek Spinach Pies

These little horns of filo pastry are stuffed with a simple spinach and feta cheese filling to make a quick and easy main course.

SERVES 8
225 g/8 oz fresh leaf spinach
2 spring onions, chopped
175 g/6 oz feta cheese, crumbled
1 egg, beaten
15 ml/1 tbsp fresh dill, chopped
ground black pepper
4 large sheets or 8 small sheets of filo
    pastry
olive oil, for brushing

COOK'S TIP

The pies can be prepared ahead and chilled for a day or two, before baking and serving warm. Alternatively, open freeze on a wire rack, then wrap well in foil or cling film and freeze for up to one month. Uncover and thaw well before baking as the recipe above.

1 Preheat the oven to 190°C/375°F/ Gas 5. Blanch the spinach in the tiniest amount of water until just wilted, then drain very well, pressing it through a sieve with the back of a wooden spoon.

2 Chop the spinach finely and mix with the onions, feta, egg, dill and ground black pepper.

3 Lay out a sheet of filo pastry and brush with olive oil. If large, cut the pieces in two and sandwich them together. If small, fit another sheet on top and brush with olive oil.

4 Spread a quarter of the filling on one edge of the filo at the bottom, then roll it up firmly, but not too tightly. Shape into a crescent and place on a baking sheet.

5 Brush the pastry well with oil and bake for about 20–25 minutes in the preheated oven until golden and crisp. Cool slightly then remove to a wire rack to cool further.

Chunky Vegetable Paella

This Spanish rice dish has become a firm family favourite the world over. There are very many versions: here is one with aubergine and chick peas.

SERVES 6
good pinch saffron strands
1 aubergine, cut in thick chunks
salt
90 ml/6 tbsp olive oil
1 large onion, sliced
3 garlic cloves, crushed
1 yellow pepper, sliced
1 red pepper, sliced
10 ml/2 tsp paprika
225 g/8 oz/1¼ cups risotto rice
600 ml/1 pint/2½ cups stock
450 g/1 lb fresh tomatoes, skinned and
    chopped
ground black pepper
115 g/4 oz sliced mushrooms
115 g/4 oz cut green beans
1 × 400 g/14 oz can chick peas

1 Steep the saffron in 45 ml/3 tbsp hot water. Sprinkle the aubergine with salt, leave to drain in a colander for 30 minutes, then rinse and dry.

2 In a large paella or frying pan, heat the oil and fry the onion, garlic, peppers and aubergine for about 5 minutes, stirring occasionally. Sprinkle in the paprika and stir again.

3 Mix in the rice, then pour in the stock, tomatoes, saffron and seasoning. Bring to a boil then simmer for 15 minutes, uncovered, shaking the pan frequently and stirring occasionally.

4 Stir in the mushrooms, green beans and chick peas (with the liquor). Continue cooking for a further 10 minutes, then serve hot from the pan.

Green Lentil Kulbyaka

This traditional Russian dish, usually made with fish and dough, can be adapted to make a light, crisp vegetarian centrepiece using filo pastry and green lentils.

SERVES 6

175 g/6 oz/1 cup green lentils, soaked for 30 minutes
2 bay leaves
2 onions, sliced
1.2 litres/2 pints/5 cups stock
175 g/6 oz/¾ cup butter, melted
225 g/8 oz/1¼ cups long grain rice, ideally basmati
salt and ground black pepper
60 ml/4 tbsp fresh parsley, chopped
30 ml/2 tbsp fresh dill, chopped
1 egg, beaten
225 g/8 oz mushrooms, sliced
about 8 sheets filo pastry
3 eggs, hard-boiled and sliced

1 Drain the lentils then simmer with the bay leaves, one onion and half the stock for 25 minutes until cooked and thick. Season well, cool and set aside.

VARIATION

You could use a vegetarian puff pastry. In this case, use two blocks of pastry, placing one on top of the other and rolling to a large rectangle. Alternatively, you could make two separate kulbyakas. Divide the filling between the pastry and seal the edges well, glazing the tops with beaten egg.

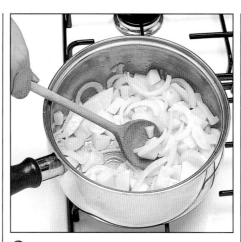

2 Gently fry the remaining onion in another saucepan with 30 ml/2 tbsp of the butter for 5 minutes. Stir in the rice then the rest of the stock.

3 Season, bring to the boil, then cover and cook gently for 12 minutes for basmati, 15 minutes for long grain. Leave to stand, uncovered for 5 minutes then stir in the fresh herbs. Cool, then beat in the raw egg.

4 Fry the mushrooms in 45 ml/3 tbsp of the butter for 5 minutes until they are just soft. Cool and set aside.

5 Brush the inside of a large, shallow ovenproof dish with more butter. Lay the sheets of filo in it, covering the base and making sure most of the pastry overhangs the sides. Brush well with butter in between and overlapping the pastry as required. Ensure there is a lot of pastry to fold over the mounded filling.

6 Into the pastry lining, layer rice, lentils and mushrooms, repeating the layers at least once and tucking the sliced egg in between. Season as you layer and form an even mound of filling.

7 Bring up the sheets of pastry over the filling, scrunching the top into attractive folds. Brush all over with the rest of the butter and set aside to chill and firm up.

8 Preheat the oven to 190°C/375°F/ Gas 5. When ready, bake the kulbyaka for about 45 minutes until golden and crisp. Allow to stand for 10 minutes before you cut it and serve.

Chilli con Queso 🌿

Known as a 'bowl of red', this classic Mexican dish is just as tasty when made with all-red beans. For an extra good flavour, use small cubes of smoked cheese, and serve with rice. Epazote is a traditional Mexican herb found in specialist stores.

SERVES 4
225 g/8 oz/2 cups red kidney beans, soaked and drained
45 ml/3 tbsp sunflower oil
1 onion, chopped
1 red pepper, chopped
2 garlic cloves, crushed
1 fresh red chilli, chopped (optional)
15 ml/1 tbsp chilli powder (mild or hot)
5 ml/1 tsp ground cumin
1 litre/1¾ pints/4 cups stock or water
5 ml/1 tsp crushed dried epazote leaves (optional)
ground black pepper
salt
15 g/½ oz granulated sugar
115 g/4 oz cheese, cubed, to serve

1 Rinse the beans. In a large saucepan heat the oil and gently fry the onion, pepper, garlic and fresh chilli for about 5 minutes.

2 Stir in the spices and cook for another minute, then add the beans, stock or water, epazote (if using) and a grinding of pepper. Don't add salt at this stage.

3 Boil for 10 minutes, cover and turn down to a gentle simmer. Cook for about 50 minutes checking the water level and adding extra if necessary.

4 When the beans are tender, season them well with salt. Remove about a quarter of the mixture and mash to a pulp or pass through a food processor.

5 Return the purée to the pan and stir well. Add sugar and serve hot with the cheese sprinkled on top. Great with plain boiled long grain rice.

Big Barley Bowl

Barley seems to have slipped from fashion in recent years – a pity as it is a delicious grain with a marvellous nutty texture. Serve this with crisp cheesy croûtes.

SERVES 6
1 red onion, sliced
½ fennel bulb, sliced
2 carrots, cut in sticks
1 parsnip, sliced
45 ml/3 tbsp sunflower oil
115 g/4 oz/1 cup pearl barley
1 litre/1¼ pints/4 cups stock
5 ml/1 tsp dried thyme
fresh parsley, chopped, to garnish
salt and ground black pepper
115 g/4 oz/⅔ cup green beans, sliced
1 × 425 g/15 oz can pinto beans, drained
CROÛTES
1 medium sized baguette, sliced
olive oil, for brushing
1 garlic clove, cut in half
60 ml/4 tbsp grated Parmesan cheese

1 In a large, heatproof casserole, sauté the onion, fennel, carrots and parsnip gently in the oil for 10 minutes.

2 Stir in the barley and stock. Bring to a boil, add the herbs and seasoning, then cover and simmer gently for 40 minutes.

3 Stir in the green beans and pinto beans and continue cooking – covered – for a further 20 minutes.

4 Meanwhile, preheat the oven to 190°C/375°F/Gas 5. Brush the baguette slices with olive oil and place them on a baking sheet.

5 Bake for about 15 minutes until light golden and crisp. Remove from the oven and quickly rub each croûte with the garlic halves. Sprinkle over the cheese and return to the oven to melt.

6 Ladle the barley into warm bowls and serve sprinkled with parsley, accompanied by the cheesy croûtes. This dish is nicest eaten with a spoon.

Vegetables Julienne with a Red Pepper Coulis

Just the right course for those watching their weight. Choose a selection of as many vegetables as you feel you can eat. Cut them into equal size finger lengths and steam them over aromatic, bubbling water.

SERVES 2

A selection of vegetables. Choose from:
  carrots, turnips, asparagus, parsnips,
  courgettes, green beans, broccoli,
  salsify, cauliflower, mangetouts

RED PEPPER COULIS
1 small onion, chopped
1 garlic clove, crushed
15 ml/1 tbsp sunflower oil
15 ml/1 tbsp water
3 red peppers, roasted, skinned and
  chopped
120 ml/8 tbsp fromage frais
squeeze of fresh lemon juice
salt and ground black pepper
sprigs of fresh thyme
2 bay leaves
fresh green herbs, to garnish

1 Prepare the vegetables by cutting them into thin fingers or small, bite size pieces.

2 Make the coulis: lightly sauté the onion and garlic in the oil and water for 3 minutes then add the peppers and cook for a further 2 minutes.

3 Pass the coulis through a food processor, then work in the fromage frais, lemon juice and seasoning.

4 Boil some salted water with the fresh thyme and bay leaves, and fit a steamer over the top.

5 Arrange the prepared vegetables on the steamer, placing the harder root vegetables at the bottom and steaming these for about 3 minutes.

6 Add the other vegetables according to their natural tenderness and cook for a further 2–4 minutes.

7 Serve the vegetables on plates with the sauce to one side. Garnish with fresh green herbs, if you wish.

VARIATION

The red pepper coulis makes a wonderful sauce for many other dishes. Try it spooned over fresh pasta with lightly steamed or fried courgettes, or use it as a pouring sauce for savoury filled crêpes.

Curried Parsnip Pie

Sweet, creamy parsnips are beautifully complemented by the addition of curry spices and cheese. This unusual but delicious combination of flavours makes for a very tasty pie.

SERVES 4

PASTRY
115 g/4 oz/8 tbsp butter or margarine
225 g/8 oz/1 cup plain flour
salt and ground black pepper
5 ml/1 tsp dried thyme or oregano
cold water, to mix

FILLING
8 baby onions, or shallots, peeled
2 large parsnips, thinly sliced
2 carrots, thinly sliced
25 g/1 oz/2 tbsp butter or margarine
30 ml/2 tbsp wholemeal flour
15 ml/1 tbsp mild curry or tikka paste
300 ml/½ pint/1¼ cups milk
115 g/4 oz mature cheese, grated
salt and ground black pepper
45 ml/3 tbsp fresh coriander or parsley, chopped
1 egg yolk, beaten with 10 ml/2 tsp water

1 Make the pastry by rubbing the butter or margarine into the flour until it resembles fine breadcrumbs. Season and stir in the thyme or oregano, then mix to a firm dough with cold water.

2 Blanch the baby onions or shallots with the parsnips and carrots in just enough water to cover, for about 5 minutes. Drain, reserving about 300 ml/ ½ pint/1¼ cups of the liquid.

3 In a clean pan, melt the butter or margarine, and stir in the flour and spice paste to make a roux. Gradually whisk in the reserved stock and milk until smooth. Simmer for a minute or two.

4 Take the pan off the heat, stir in the cheese and seasoning, then mix into the vegetables with the coriander or parsley.

COOK'S TIP

This pie freezes well and makes a good stand-by for a mid-week meal. For best results, make up to the final stage and freeze unbaked. Open freeze until solid, then wrap well in freezer cling film, seal and label. Use within one month.

Cauliflower, broccoli or any other favourite vegetable can be added to the filling to give a variety of flavours and textures.

5 Pour into a pie dish, fix a pie funnel in the centre and allow to cool.

6 Roll out the pastry, large enough to fit the top of the pie dish. Re-roll the trimmings into long strips.

7 Brush the pastry edges with egg yolk wash and fit on the pastry strips. Brush again with egg yolk wash.

8 Using a rolling pin, lift the rolled out pastry over the pie top and fit over the funnel, pressing it down well onto the strips underneath.

9 Cut off the overhanging pastry and crimp the edges. Cut a hole for the funnel, brush all over well with the remaining egg yolk wash and make decorations with the trimmings, glazing them too.

10 Place the pie dish on a baking sheet and chill for 30 minutes while you preheat the oven to 200°C/400°F/Gas 6. Bake the pie for about 25–30 minutes until golden brown and crisp on top.

made with Monteuay Jack Cheese — TRY another kind eliminate Thyme

Vegetables under a Light Creamy Crust

This light main course dish is ideal for a summer supper. The subtle flavours of leeks, courgettes and mushrooms are topped by a tasty crust of fromage frais, cheese and breadcrumbs.

SERVES 4
2 leeks, thinly sliced
3 courgettes, thickly sliced *—Zucchinni*
350 g/12 oz sliced mushrooms, including oyster and shitake mushrooms
2 garlic cloves, crushed
30 ml/2 tbsp olive oil
25 g/1 oz/2 tbsp butter
15 ml/1 tbsp plain flour
300 ml/½ pint/1¼ cups stock
5 ml/1 tsp dried thyme
salt and ground black pepper
30 ml/2 tbsp fromage frais *—Cheese*
TOPPING
450 g/1 lb fromage frais
25 g/1 oz/2 tbsp butter, melted
3 eggs, beaten
salt and ground black pepper
fresh nutmeg, grated
freshly grated cheese and dried breadcrumbs, to sprinkle

1 Preheat the oven to 190°C/375°F/Gas 5. In a saucepan, gently fry the leeks, courgettes, mushrooms and garlic in the oil and butter for about 7 minutes, stirring occasionally, until the vegetables are just soft.

2 Stir in the flour then gradually mix in the stock. Bring to a boil, stirring until thickened. Add the thyme and seasoning. Take the pan off the heat and stir in the fromage frais. Pour the vegetable mixture into a shallow ovenproof dish.

3 Beat the topping ingredients together, seasoning them well and adding the nutmeg to taste. Spoon on top of the vegetables and sprinkle with cheese and breadcrumbs.

4 Bake for about 30 minutes until a light golden, firm crust forms. Serve hot with pasta or crusty bread.

Potato and Parsnip Amandine

Shells of baked potatoes are filled with a spicy parsnip and crunchy almond mix. They make an unusual alternative to plain jacket potatoes.

SERVES 4
4 large baking potatoes
olive oil, for greasing
225 g/8 oz parsnips, diced
25 g/1 oz/2 tbsp butter
5 ml/1 tsp cumin seeds
5 ml/1 tsp ground coriander
30 ml/2 tbsp single cream or natural yogurt
salt and ground black pepper
115 g/4 oz Gruyère or Cheddar cheese, grated
1 egg, beaten
50 g/2 oz/¼ cup flaked almonds

1 Rub the potatoes all over with oil, score in half, then bake at 200°C/400°F/Gas 6 for about 1 hour until cooked.

2 Meanwhile, boil the parsnips until tender, then drain well, mash and mix with the butter, spices and cream or natural yogurt.

3 When the potatoes are cooked, halve, scoop out and mash the flesh then mix with the parsnip, seasoning well.

4 Stir in the cheese, egg and three quarters of the almonds. Fill the potato shells with the mixture and sprinkle over the remaining almonds.

5 Return to the oven and bake for about 15–20 minutes until golden brown and the filling has set lightly. Serve hot with a side salad.

Autumn Glory

Glorious pumpkin shells summon up the delights of autumn and seem too good simply to throw away. Use one instead as a serving pot. Pumpkin and pasta make marvellous partners, especially as a main course served from the baked shell.

SERVES 4
1 × 2 kg/4 lb pumpkin
1 onion, sliced
2.5 cm/1 in cube fresh root ginger
45 ml/3 tbsp extra virgin olive oil
1 courgette, sliced
115 g/4 oz sliced mushrooms
1 × 400 g/14 oz can chopped tomatoes
75 g/3 oz/1 cup pasta shells
450 ml/¾ pint/2 cups stock
salt and ground black pepper
60 ml/4 tbsp fromage frais
30 ml/2 tbsp fresh basil, chopped

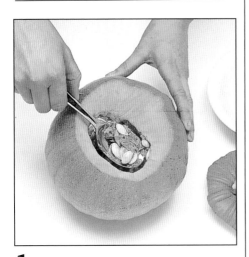

1 Preheat the oven to 180°C/350°F/Gas 4. Cut the top off the pumpkin with a large, sharp knife and scoop out and discard the seeds.

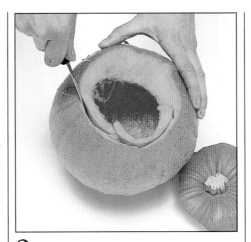

2 Using a small sharp knife and a sturdy tablespoon extract as much of the pumpkin flesh as possible, then chop it into chunks.

3 Bake the pumpkin with its lid on for 45 minutes to one hour until the inside begins to soften.

4 Meanwhile, make the filling. Gently fry the onion, ginger and pumpkin flesh in the olive oil for about 10 minutes, stirring occasionally.

5 Add the courgette and mushrooms and cook for a further 3 minutes, then stir in the tomatoes, pasta shells and stock. Season well, bring to a boil, then cover and simmer gently for 10 minutes.

6 Stir the fromage frais and basil into the pasta and spoon the mixture into the pumpkin. (It may not be possible to fit all the filling into the pumpkin shell, so serve the rest separately if this is the case.)

Festive Lentil and Nut Roast

An excellent celebration mould which can be served with all the trimmings, including vegetarian gravy. Garnish it with fresh cranberries and French parsley for a really festive effect.

SERVES 6–8
115 g/4 oz/⅔ cup red lentils
115 g/4 oz/1 cup hazelnuts
115 g/4 oz/1 cup walnuts
1 large carrot
2 celery sticks
1 large onion
115 g/4 oz mushrooms
50 g/2 oz/4 tbsp butter
10 ml/2 tsp mild curry powder
30 ml/2 tbsp tomato ketchup
30 ml/2 tbsp Worcestershire sauce
1 egg, beaten
10 ml/2 tsp salt
60 ml/4 tbsp fresh parsley, chopped
150 ml/¼ pint/⅔ cup water

1 Soak the lentils for 1 hour in cold water then drain well. Grind the nuts in a food processor until quite fine but not too smooth. Set the nuts aside.

2 Chop the carrot, celery, onion and mushrooms into small chunks, then pass them through a food processor or blender until they are quite finely chopped.

3 Fry the vegetables gently in the butter for 5 minutes then stir in the curry powder and cook for a minute. Cool.

4 Meanwhile, mix the soaked lentils with the nuts, vegetables, ketchup, Worcestershire sauce, egg, salt, parsley and water.

5 Grease and line the base and sides of a long 1 kg/2 lb loaf tin with greaseproof paper or a sheet of foil. Press the mixture into the tin. Preheat the oven to 190°C/375°F/Gas 5.

6 Bake for about 1–1¼ hours until just firm, covering the top with a butter paper or piece of foil if it starts to burn.

7 Allow the mixture to stand for about 15 minutes before you turn it out and peel off the paper. It will be fairly soft when cut as it is a moist loaf.

Vegetarian Gravy

Make up a large batch of this and freeze it in small containers ready to reheat and serve. A delicious alternative to the meaty version.

MAKES ABOUT 1 LITRE/1¾ PINTS
1 large red onion, sliced
3 turnips, sliced
3 celery sticks, sliced
115 g/4 oz mushrooms, halved
2 whole garlic cloves
90 ml/6 tbsp sunflower oil
1.5 litres/2½ pints/6 cups vegetable stock
  or water
45 ml/3 tbsp soy sauce
good pinch of granulated sugar
salt and ground black pepper

1 Cook the vegetables and garlic on a moderately high heat with the oil in a large saucepan, stirring occasionally until nicely browned but not singed. This should take about 15–20 minutes.

2 Add the stock or water and soy sauce, bring to the boil then cover and simmer for another 20 minutes.

3 Purée the vegetables, adding a little of the stock, and return them to the pan by rubbing the pulp through a sieve with the back of a ladle or wooden spoon.

4 Taste for seasoning and add the sugar. Freeze at least half of the gravy to use later and reheat the rest to serve with the lentil and nut roast.

Homemade Ravioli

It is a pleasure to make your own fresh pasta and you might be surprised at just how easy it is to fill and shape ravioli. Allow a little extra time than you would for ready-made or dried pasta. A food processor will save you time and effort in making and kneading the dough. A pasta rolling machine helps with the rolling out, but both these jobs can be done by hand if necessary.

SERVES 6
200 g/7 oz/1½ cups strong plain flour
5 ml/½ tsp salt
15 ml/1 tbsp olive oil
2 eggs, beaten
FILLING
1 small red onion, finely chopped
1 small green pepper, finely chopped
1 carrot, coarsely grated
15 ml/1 tbsp olive oil
50 g/2 oz/½ cup walnuts, chopped
115 g/4 oz ricotta cheese
30 ml/2 tbsp fresh Parmesan or Pecorino
  cheese, grated
15 ml/1 tbsp fresh marjoram or basil,
  chopped
salt and ground black pepper
extra oil or melted butter, to serve

1 Sift the flour and salt into a food processor. With the machine running, trickle in the oil and eggs and blend to a stiff but smooth dough.

2 Allow the machine to run for at least a minute if possible, otherwise remove the dough and knead it by hand for 5 minutes.

3 If you are using a pasta machine, break off small balls of dough and then feed them through the rollers, several times, according to the machine manufacturer's instructions.

4 If rolling the pasta by hand, divide the dough into two and roll out on a lightly floured surface to a thickness of about 6 mm/¼ in.

5 Fold the pasta into three and re-roll. Repeat this up to six times until the dough is smooth and no longer sticky. Roll the pasta slightly more thinly each time.

6 Keep the rolled dough under clean, dry tea towels while you complete the rest and make the filling. You should aim to have an even number of pasta sheets, all the same size if rolling by machine.

7 Fry the onion, pepper and carrot in the oil for 5 minutes, then allow to cool. Mix with the walnuts, cheeses, herbs and seasoning.

8 Lay out a pasta sheet and place small scoops of the filling in neat rows about 5 cm/2 in apart. Brush in between with a little water and then place another pasta sheet on the top.

9 Press down well in between the rows then, using a ravioli or pastry cutter, cut into squares. If the edges pop open occasionally, press them back gently with your fingers.

10 Leave the ravioli to dry in the refrigerator, then boil in plenty of lightly salted water for just 5 minutes.

11 Toss the cooked ravioli in a little oil or melted butter before serving with homemade tomato sauce or extra cheese.

Artichoke and Leek Crêpes

Fill thin pancakes with a mouth-watering soufflé mixture of Jerusalem artichokes and leek to serve for a special main course.

SERVES 4
115 g/4 oz/1 cup plain flour
pinch of salt
1 egg
300 ml/½ pint/1¼ cups milk
oil, for brushing
SOUFFLÉ FILLING
450 g/1 lb Jerusalem artichokes, peeled and diced
1 large leek, sliced thinly
50 g/2 oz/4 tbsp butter
30 ml/2 tbsp self-raising flour
30 ml/2 tbsp single cream
75 g/3 oz mature Cheddar cheese, grated
30 ml/2 tbsp fresh parsley, chopped
fresh nutmeg, grated
2 eggs, separated
salt and ground black pepper

1 Make the crêpe batter by blending the flour, salt, egg and milk to a smooth batter in a food processor or blender.

2 Using a crêpe or omelette pan with a diameter of about 20 cm/8 in, make a batch of thin pancakes. You will need about 30 ml/2 tbsp of batter for each one.

3 Stack the pancakes under a clean tea towel as you make them. Reserve eight for this dish and freeze the rest.

4 Cook the artichokes and leek with the butter in a covered saucepan on a gentle heat for about 12 minutes until very soft. Mash with the back of a wooden spoon. Season well.

5 Stir the flour into the vegetables and cook for 1 minute. Take the pan off the heat and beat in the cream, cheese, parsley and nutmeg to taste. Cool, then add the egg yolks.

6 Whisk the egg whites until they form soft peaks and carefully fold them into the leek/artichoke mixture.

7 Lightly grease a small ovenproof dish and preheat the oven to 190°C/375°F/Gas 5. Fold each pancake in four, hold the top open and spoon the mixture into the centre.

8 Arrange the crêpes in the prepared dish with the filling uppermost if possible. Bake for about 15 minutes until risen and golden. Eat immediately!

COOK'S TIP

Make sure the pan is at a good steady heat and is well oiled before you pour in the batter. It should sizzle as it hits the pan. Swirl the batter round to coat the pan, and then cook quickly.

Mushroom Gougère

Very good use pie plate

A savoury choux pastry ring makes a marvellous main course dish that can be made ahead then baked when required. Why not try it for a dinner party? It looks so very special.

SERVES 4
115 g/4 oz/½ cup strong plain flour
2.5 ml/½ tsp salt
75 g/3 oz/6 tbsp butter
200 ml/7 fl oz/¾ cup cold water
3 eggs, beaten — *small eggs*
75 g/3 oz/¾ cup diced Gruyère or mature
   Gouda cheese
FILLING
1 small onion, sliced
1 carrot, coarsely grated
225 g/8 oz button mushrooms, sliced
40 g/1½ oz/3 tbsp butter or margarine
5 ml/1 tsp tikka or mild curry paste *med or hot*
25 g/1 oz/2 tbsp plain flour
300 ml/½ pint/1¼ cups milk
30 ml/2 tbsp fresh parsley, chopped
salt and ground black pepper
30 ml/2 tbsp flaked almonds

---

1 Preheat the oven to 200°C/400°F/ Gas 6. Grease a shallow ovenproof dish about 23 cm/9 in long.

2 To make the choux pastry, first sift the flour and salt onto a sheet of grease-proof paper.

3 In a large saucepan, heat the butter and water until the butter just melts. Do not let the water boil. Fold the paper and shoot the flour into the pan all at once.

4 With a wooden spoon, beat the mixture rapidly until the lumps become smooth and the mixture comes away from the sides of the pan. Cool for 10 minutes.

5 Beat the eggs gradually into the mixture until you have a soft, but still quite stiff, dropping consistency. You may not need all the egg.

6 Stir in the cheese, then spoon the mixture round the sides of the greased ovenproof dish.

7 To make the filling, sauté the onion, carrot and mushrooms in the butter or margarine for 5 minutes. Stir in the curry paste then the flour.

8 Gradually stir in the milk and heat until thickened. Mix in the parsley, season well, then pour into the centre of the choux pastry.

9 Bake for 35–40 minutes until risen and golden brown, sprinkling on the almonds for the last 5 minutes or so. Serve at once.

COOK'S TIP

Choux pastry is remarkably easy to make, as no rolling out is required. The secret of success is to let the flour and butter mixture cool before beating in the eggs, to prevent them from setting.

Cabbage Roulades with Lemon Sauce

Cabbage or chard leaves filled with a rice and lentil stuffing and served with a light eggy lemon sauce makes a light and tasty main course.

SERVES 4–6

12 large cabbage or chard leaves, stalks
  removed
salt
30 ml/2 tbsp sunflower oil
1 onion, chopped
1 large carrot, grated
115 g/4 oz sliced mushrooms
600 ml/1 pint/2½ cups stock
115 g/4 oz/½ cup long grain rice
60 ml/4 tbsp red lentils
5 ml/1 tsp dried oregano or marjoram
ground black pepper
100 g/3½ oz soft cheese with garlic
SAUCE
30 g/1 oz/3 tbsp plain flour
juice of 1 lemon
3 eggs, beaten

1 Blanch the leaves in boiling, salted water until they begin to wilt. Drain, reserve the water and pat the leaves dry with kitchen paper.

2 Heat the oil and lightly fry the onion, carrot and mushrooms for 5 minutes, and then pour in the stock.

3 Add the rice, lentils, herbs and seasoning. Bring to a boil, cover and simmer gently for 15 minutes. Remove, then stir in the cheese. Preheat the oven to 190°C/375°F/Gas 5.

4 Lay out the chard or cabbage leaves rib side down, and spoon on the filling at the stalk end. Fold the sides in and roll up.

5 Place the join side down in a small roasting pan and pour in the reserved cabbage water. Cover with lightly greased foil and bake for 30–45 minutes until the leaves are tender.

6 Remove the cabbage rolls from the oven, drain and place on a serving dish. Strain 600 ml/1 pint/2½ cups of the cooking water into a saucepan and bring to a boil.

7 Blend the flour to a runny paste with a little cold water and whisk into the boiling stock, together with the lemon juice.

8 Beat the eggs in a heatproof jug and slowly pour on the hot stock, whisking well as you go.

9 Return to the stove and on the lowest heat, stir until smooth and thick. Do not allow the sauce to boil or it will curdle. Serve the rolls with some of the sauce poured over and the rest handed separately.

Irish Colcannon

This lovely warming winter's dish bears a slight resemblance to Eggs Florentine. Here, baked eggs nestle among creamy potatoes with curly kale or cabbage and a topping of grated cheese.

SERVES 4
1 kg/2 lb potatoes, cut in even pieces
225 g/8 oz curly kale or crisp green
  cabbage, shredded
2 spring onions, chopped
butter or margarine, to taste
fresh nutmeg, grated
salt and ground black pepper
4 large eggs
75 g/3 oz mature cheese, grated

1 Boil the potatoes until just tender, then drain and mash well.

2 Lightly cook the kale or cabbage until just tender but still crisp. Preheat the oven to 190°C/375°F/Gas 5.

3 Drain the greens and mix them into the potato with the onions, butter or margarine and nutmeg. Season to taste.

4 Spoon the mixture into a shallow ovenproof dish and make four hollows in the mixture. Crack an egg into each and season well.

5 Bake for about 12 minutes or until the eggs are just set, then serve sprinkled with the cheese.

Pasta with Caponata

The Sicilians have an excellent sweet and sour vegetable dish called *caponata*, which naturally enough goes wonderfully well with pasta.

SERVES 4
1 medium aubergine, cut into sticks
2 medium courgettes, cut into sticks
8 baby onions, peeled or 1 large onion,
  sliced
2 garlic cloves, crushed
1 large red pepper, sliced
60 ml/4 tbsp olive oil, preferably extra
  virgin
450 ml/¾ pint/scant 2 cups tomato juice
  or 1 × 500 ml/17 fl oz carton creamed
  tomatoes
150 ml/¼ pint/⅔ cup water
30 ml/2 tbsp balsamic vinegar
juice of 1 lemon
15 ml/1 tbsp sugar
30 ml/2 tbsp sliced black olives
30 ml/2 tbsp capers
salt and ground black pepper
400 g/14 oz tagliatelle or other pasta
  ribbons

1 Lightly salt the aubergine and courgettes and leave them to drain in a colander for 30 minutes. Rinse and pat dry with kitchen paper towel.

2 In a large saucepan, lightly fry the onions, garlic and pepper in the oil for 5 minutes, then stir in the aubergine and courgettes and fry for a further 5 minutes.

3 Stir in the tomato juice or creamed tomatoes plus the water. Stir well, bringing the mixture to the boil, then add all the rest of the ingredients except the pasta. Season to taste and then simmer for 10 minutes.

4 Meanwhile, boil the pasta according to the instructions on the pack, then drain. Serve the caponata with the pasta.

Spinach Gnocchi

This wholesome Italian dish is ideal for making in advance then baking when required. Serve it with a fresh tomato sauce.

SERVES 4–6
400 g/14 oz fresh leaf spinach or 150 g/
  6 oz frozen leaf spinach, thawed
750 ml/1¼ pints/good 3 cups milk
200 g/7 oz/1¼ cups semolina
50 g/2 oz/4 tbsp butter, melted
50 g/2 oz Parmesan cheese, freshly
  grated, plus extra to serve
fresh nutmeg, grated
salt and ground black pepper
2 eggs, beaten

2 In a large saucepan, heat the milk and when just on the point of boiling, sprinkle in the semolina in a steady stream, stirring it briskly with a wooden spoon.

5 Stamp out shapes using a plain round cutter with a diameter of 4 cm/1½ in. Reserve the trimmings.

1 Blanch the spinach in the tiniest amount of water then drain and squeeze dry through a sieve with the back of a ladle. Chop the spinach roughly.

3 Simmer the semolina for 2 minutes then remove from the heat and stir in half the butter, most of the cheese, nutmeg and seasoning to taste and the spinach. Allow to cool for 5 minutes.

6 Grease a shallow ovenproof dish. Place the trimmings on the base and arrange the gnocchi rounds on top with each one overlapping.

7 Brush the tops with the remaining butter and sprinkle over the last of the cheese.

8 Preheat the oven when ready to bake to 190°C/375°F/Gas 5 and cook for about 35 minutes until golden and crisp on top. Serve hot with fresh tomato sauce and extra cheese.

VARIATION

For a special occasion, make half plain and half spinach gnocchi and arrange in an attractive pattern to serve. Use the same recipe as above but halve the amount of spinach and add to half the mixture in a separate bowl to make two batches. Stamp out and cook the gnocchi as normal. For a more substantial, healthy meal, make a tasty vegetable base of lightly sautéed peppers, courgettes and mushrooms and place the gnocchi on the top.

4 Stir in the eggs then tip the mixture out onto a shallow baking sheet, spreading it to a 1 cm/½ in thickness. Allow to cool completely then chill until solid.

Red Rice Rissoles

Risotto rice chills to a firm texture yet remains light and creamy when reheated as crisp crumbed rissoles. These contain small nuggets of cheese for extra creaminess.

SERVES ABOUT 8
1 large red onion, chopped
1 red pepper, chopped
2 garlic cloves, crushed
1 red chilli, finely chopped
30 ml/2 tbsp olive oil
25 g/1 oz/2 tbsp butter
225 g/8 oz/1¼ cups risotto rice
1 litre/1¾ pints/4½ cups stock
4 sun-dried tomatoes, chopped
30 ml/2 tbsp tomato purée
10 ml/2 tsp dried oregano
salt and ground black pepper
45 ml/3 tbsp fresh parsley, chopped
150 g/6 oz cheese, e.g. Red Leicester or
    smoked Cheddar
1 egg, beaten
115 g/4 oz/1 cup dried breadcrumbs
oil, for deep frying

1 Fry the onion, pepper, garlic and chilli in the oil and butter for 5 minutes. Stir in the rice and fry for a further 2 minutes.

2 Pour in the stock and add the tomatoes, purée, oregano and seasoning. Bring to the boil, stirring occasionally, then cover and simmer for 20 minutes.

3 Stir in the parsley then turn into a shallow dish, cool and chill until firm. When cold, divide into 12 and shape into balls.

4 Cut the cheese into 12 pieces and press a nugget into the centre of each of the rissoles.

5 Put the beaten egg in one bowl and the breadcrumbs into another. Dip the rissoles first into the egg then into the breadcrumbs, coating each one evenly.

6 Lay the coated rissoles on a plate and chill again for 30 minutes. Fill a deep fat frying pan one-third full of oil and heat until a cube of day-old bread browns in under a minute.

7 Fry the rissoles in batches, reheating the oil in between, for about 3–4 minutes. Drain on kitchen paper and keep warm, uncovered, before serving.

Broad Bean and Cauliflower Curry

A tasty mid-week curry to serve with rice (especially a brown basmati), small popadums and maybe a cucumber raita.

SERVES 4
2 garlic cloves, chopped
2.5 cm/1 in cube fresh root ginger
1 fresh green chilli, seeded and chopped
15 ml/1 tbsp oil
1 onion, sliced
1 large potato, chopped
30 ml/2 tbsp ghee or softened butter
15 ml/1 tbsp curry powder, mild or hot
1 medium size cauliflower, cut into small florets
600 ml/1 pint/2½ cups stock
25 g/1 oz/2 tbsp creamed coconut
salt and ground black pepper
1 × 285 g/10 oz can broad beans, with liquor
juice of half a lemon (optional)
fresh coriander or parsley, chopped, to serve

1 Blend the garlic, ginger, chilli and oil in a food processor until they form a smooth paste.

2 In a large saucepan, fry the onion and potato in the ghee or butter for 5 minutes then stir in the spice paste and curry powder. Cook for 1 minute.

3 Add the cauliflower florets and stir well into the spicy mixture, then pour in the stock. Bring to a boil and mix in the coconut, stirring until it melts.

4 Season well then cover and simmer for 10 minutes. Add the beans and their liquor and cook uncovered for a further 10 minutes.

5 Check the seasoning and add a good squeeze of lemon juice if liked. Serve hot garnished with coriander or parsley.

SALADS & VEGETABLE DISHES

Here is a delightful range of colourful salads and scrumptious
vegetable dishes and accompaniments. Varied but easy to obtain
ingredients ensure the perfect recipe for every style of meal.

Bean Sprout Stir-fry

Homegrown bean sprouts taste so good, tossed into a tasty stir-fry. They have more flavour and texture than shop bought varieties and are very nutritious, being rich in vitamins and high in fibre. (Old dried beans will not sprout, so use beans that are well within their 'Use by' date.)

SERVES 3–4

30 ml/2 tbsp sunflower or groundnut oil
225 g/8 oz mixed sprouted beans
2 spring onions, chopped
1 garlic clove, crushed
30 ml/2 tbsp soy sauce
10 ml/2 tsp sesame oil
15 ml/1 tbsp sesame seeds
30 ml/2 tbsp fresh coriander or parsley, chopped
salt and ground black pepper

1 Heat the sunflower or groundnut oil in a large wok and stir-fry the sprouting beans, onion and garlic for 3–5 minutes.

2 Add the remaining ingredients, cook for 1–2 minutes more and serve hot.

HOME SPROUTING BEANS

Use any of the following pulses to grow your own sprouts: green or brown lentils, aduki beans, mung beans, chick peas, flageolet and haricot beans, soya beans or Indian massor dal.

Cover 45 ml/3 tbsp of your chosen pulses with lukewarm water. Leave to soak overnight, then drain and rinse.

Place in a large clean jam jar or special sprouting tray. Cover with muslin and secure with a rubber band. If using a jam jar, lay the jar on its side and shake it so the beans spread along the length. Leave somewhere warm.

Rinse the beans night and morning with plenty of cold water, running this through the muslin, and drain. Carefully place the jar back on its side.

Repeat this twice a day until roots and shoots appear. (If nothing happens after 48 hours, the beans are probably too old.) When the shoots are at least twice the length of the bean, rinse finally and store in the fridge for up to two days.

Panzanella Salad

If sliced juicy tomatoes layered with day old bread sounds strange for a salad, don't be deceived – it's quite delicious. A popular Italian salad, this dish is ideal as a starter or an accompaniment. Use full-flavoured tomatoes for the best result.

SERVES 4–6

4 thick slices day-old bread, either white, brown or rye
1 small red onion, thinly sliced
450 g/1 lb ripe tomatoes, thinly sliced
115 g/4 oz Mozzarella cheese, thinly sliced
5 ml/1 tbsp fresh basil, shredded, or marjoram
salt and ground black pepper
120 ml/4 fl oz/½ cup extra virgin olive oil
45 ml/3 tbsp balsamic vinegar
juice of 1 small lemon
stoned and sliced black olives or salted capers, to garnish

1 Dip the bread briefly in cold water, then carefully squeeze out the excess water. Arrange on the bottom of a shallow salad bowl.

2 Soak the onion slices in cold water for about 10 minutes while you prepare the other ingredients. Drain and reserve.

3 Layer the tomatoes, cheese, onion, basil or marjoram, seasoning well in between each layer. Sprinkle with oil, vinegar and lemon juice.

4 Top with the olives or capers, cover with cling film and chill in the refrigerator overnight, if possible.

Caesar's Salad

On Independence Day 1924, in Tijuana, Mexico, a restauranteur – Caesar Cardini – created this masterpiece of new American cuisine. It has all the elements of a good salad – being light, flavoursome, attractive and nutritious with a good crunch.

SERVES 4
2 thick slices crustless bread
2 garlic cloves
sunflower oil, for frying
1 Cos lettuce, torn in pieces
50 g/2 oz/½ cup fresh Parmesan cheese, coarsely grated
2 eggs
DRESSING
30 ml/2 tbsp extra virgin olive oil
10 ml/2 tsp French mustard
10 ml/2 tsp Worcestershire sauce
30 ml/2 tbsp fresh lemon juice

1 Cut the bread into cubes. Heat one of the garlic cloves slowly in about 45 ml/ 3 tbsp of the sunflower oil in a saucepan then toss in the bread cubes. Remove the garlic clove.

2 Heat an oven to 190°C/375°F/Gas 5. Spread the garlicky cubes on a baking sheet and bake the bread for about 10–12 minutes until golden and crisp. Remove and allow to cool.

3 Rub the inside of a large salad bowl with the remaining garlic clove and then discard it.

4 Toss in the torn lettuce, sprinkling between the leaves with the cheese. Cover and set the salad aside.

5 Boil a small saucepan of water and cook the eggs for 1 minute only. Remove the eggs, and crack them open into a jug or bowl. The whites should be milky and the yolks raw.

6 Whisk the dressing ingredients into the eggs. When ready to serve pour the dressing over the leaves, toss well together and serve topped with the croûtons.

VARIATION

Why not try a refreshing Italian version of this salad? Use cubed ciabatta bread for the croûtons. Rub the inside of a salad bowl with garlic and spoon in 30–45 ml/ 2–3 tbsp of good olive oil. Add a selection of torn salad leaves, including rocket, together with some shaved Parmesan cheese. Do not mix yet. Just before serving, add the croûtons, season well, then toss the leaves with the oil, coating well. Finally squeeze over the juice of a fresh lemon.

Chef's Salad

This is basically whatever you make of it – a lovely large salad containing all your favourite ingredients. It is also a good opportunity to use up leftover vegetables and small pieces of cheese from the refrigerator. For these reasons, quantities are approximate.

SERVES 6
450 g/1 lb new potatoes, halved if large
2 carrots, grated coarsely
½ small fennel bulb or 2 sticks celery, sliced thinly
50 g/2 oz sliced button mushrooms
¼ cucumber, sliced or chopped
small green or red pepper, sliced
60 ml/4 tbsp garden peas
200 g/7 oz/1 cup cooked pulses, e.g. red kidney beans or green lentils
1 Ice Gem or baby lettuce or 1 head chicory (endive)
2–3 hard boiled eggs, quartered and/or grated cheese, to serve
½ carton salad cress, snipped

1 Put all the vegetables and pulses (except the lettuce or chicory) into a large mixing bowl.

DRESSING
60 ml/4 tbsp mayonnaise
45 ml/3 tbsp natural yogurt
30 ml/2 tbsp milk
30 ml/2 tbsp chopped fresh chives or spring onion tops
salt and ground black pepper

2 Line a large platter with the lettuce or chicory leaves – creating a nest for the other salad ingredients. Mix the dressing ingredients together and pour over the salad in the mixing bowl.

3 Toss the salad thoroughly in the dressing, season well then pile into the centre of the lettuce nest.

4 Top the salad with the eggs, cheese or both and sprinkle with the snipped cress. Serve lightly chilled.

Potato and Radish Salad

So many potato salads are dressed in thick sauce. This one is quite light and colourful with a flavoursome yet delicate dressing.

SERVES 4–6
450 g/1 lb new potatoes, scrubbed
45 ml/3 tbsp olive oil
15 ml/1 tbsp walnut or hazelnut oil (optional)
30 ml/2 tbsp wine vinegar
10 ml/2 tsp coarse grain mustard
5 ml/1 tsp clear honey
salt and ground black pepper
about 6–8 radishes, thinly sliced
30 ml/2 tbsp fresh chives, chopped

1 Boil the potatoes until just tender. Drain, return to the pan and cut any large potatoes in half.

2 Make a dressing with the oils, vinegar, mustard, honey and seasoning. Mix them together thoroughly in a bowl.

3 Toss the dressing into the potatoes while they are still cooling and allow them to stand for an hour or so.

4 Mix in the radishes and chives, chill lightly, toss again and serve.

COOK'S TIP

The secret of a good potato salad is to dress the potatoes while still warm in a vinaigrette-style dressing in order to let them soak up the flavour as they cool. You can then mix in an additional creamy dressing of mayonnaise and natural yogurt if liked. Sliced celery, red onion and chopped walnuts would make a good alternative to the radishes and, for best effect, serve on a platter lined with frilly lettuce leaves.

Thai Rice and Sprouting Beans

Thai rice has a delicate fragrance and texture that is delicious whether served hot or cold. This salad is a colourful collection of popular Thai flavours and textures.

SERVES 6
30 ml/2 tbsp sesame oil
30 ml/2 tbsp fresh lime juice
1 small fresh red chilli, seeded and chopped
1 garlic clove, crushed
10 ml/2 tsp grated fresh root ginger
30 ml/2 tbsp light soy sauce
5 ml/1 tsp clear honey
45 ml/3 tbsp pineapple juice
15 ml/1 tbsp wine vinegar
225 g/8 oz/1¼ cups Thai fragrant rice, boiled
2 spring onions, sliced
2 rings canned pineapple in natural juice, chopped
150 g/5 oz/1¼ cups sprouted lentils or bean sprouts
1 small red pepper, sliced
1 stick celery, sliced
50 g/2 oz/½ cup unsalted cashew nuts, roughly chopped
30 ml/2 tbsp toasted sesame seeds
salt and ground black pepper

1 Whisk together the sesame oil, lime juice, chilli, garlic, ginger, soy sauce, honey, pineapple juice and vinegar in a large bowl. Stir in the lightly boiled rice.

2 Toss in all the remaining ingredients and mix well. This dish can be served warm or lightly chilled. If the rice grains stick together on cooling, simply stir them with a metal spoon.

Chicory, Carrot and Rocket Salad

A bright and colourful salad which is ideal for a buffet or barbecue party. Use watercress if you are unable to obtain any rocket.

SERVES 4–6
3 carrots, coarsely grated
about 50 g/2 oz fresh rocket or watercress, roughly chopped
1 large head chicory
DRESSING:
45 ml/3 tbsp sunflower oil
15 ml/1 tbsp hazelnut or walnut oil (optional)
30 ml/2 tbsp cider or wine vinegar
10 ml/2 tsp clear honey
5 ml/1 tsp grated lemon rind
15 ml/1 tbsp poppy seeds
salt and ground black pepper

1 Mix the carrot and rocket or watercress together in a large bowl and season well.

2 Shake the dressing ingredients together in a screw-topped jar then pour onto the carrot and greenery. Toss the salad thoroughly.

3 Line a shallow salad bowl with the chicory leaves and spoon the salad into the centre. Serve lightly chilled.

Bountiful Bean and Nut Salad 🍃

This is a good multi-purpose dish. It can be a cold main course, a buffet party dish, or a salad on the side. It also keeps well for up to three days in the refrigerator.

SERVES 6

75 g/3 oz/½ cup red kidney, pinto or
   borlotti beans
75 g/3 oz/½ cup white cannellini or butter
   beans
30 ml/2 tbsp olive oil
175 g/6 oz cut fresh green beans
3 spring onions, sliced
1 small yellow or red pepper, sliced
1 carrot, coarsely grated
30 ml/2 tbsp dried topping onions or
   sun-dried tomatoes, chopped
50 g/2 oz/½ cup unsalted cashew nuts or
   almonds, split

DRESSING

45 ml/3 tbsp sunflower oil
30 ml/2 tbsp red wine vinegar
15 ml/1 tbsp coarse grain mustard
5 ml/1 tsp caster sugar
5 ml/1 tsp dried mixed herbs
salt and ground black pepper

1 Soak the beans, overnight if possible, then drain and rinse well, cover with a lot of cold water and cook according to the instructions on the pack.

2 When cooked, drain and season the beans and toss them in the olive oil. Leave to cool for 30 minutes.

3 In a large bowl, mix in the other vegetables, including the sun-dried tomatoes but not the crisp topping onions, if using, or the nuts.

4 Make up the dressing by shaking all the ingredients together in a screw topped jar. Toss the dressing into the salad and check the seasoning again. Serve sprinkled with the topping onions, if using, and the split nuts.

Garden Salad and Garlic Crostini

Dress a colourful mixture of salad leaves with good olive oil and freshly squeezed lemon juice, then top it with crispy bread crostini.

SERVES 4–6
3 thick slices day old bread, e.g. ciabatta
120 ml/4 fl oz/½ cup extra virgin olive oil
garlic clove, cut
½ small Cos or Romaine lettuce
½ small oak leaf lettuce
25 g/1 oz rocket leaves or cress
25 g/1 oz fresh flat leaf parsley
a few leaves and flowers of nasturtium
flowers of pansy and pot marigold
a small handful of young dandelion
   leaves
sea salt flakes and ground black pepper
juice of 1 fresh lemon

1 Cut the bread into medium size dice about 1 cm/½ in square.

2 Heat half the oil gently in a frying pan and fry the bread cubes in it, tossing them until they are well coated and lightly browned. Remove and cool.

3 Rub the inside of a large salad bowl with the garlic and discard. Pour the rest of the oil into the bottom of the bowl.

4 Wash, dry and tear the leaves into bite size pieces and pile them into the bowl. Season with salt and pepper. Cover and keep chilled until ready to serve.

5 To serve, toss the leaves in the oil at the bottom of the bowl, then sprinkle with the lemon juice and toss again. Scatter over the crostini and serve immediately.

Californian Vim and Vit Salad

Full of vitality and vitamins, this is a lovely light healthy salad for sunny days when you feel full of energy, or need an extra boost.

SERVES 4
1 small crisp lettuce, torn in pieces
225 g/8 oz young spinach leaves
2 carrots, coarsely grated
115 g/4 oz cherry tomatoes, halved
2 celery sticks, thinly sliced
75 g/3 oz/½ cup raisins
50 g/2 oz/½ cup blanched almonds or
    unsalted cashew nuts, halved
30 ml/2 tbsp sunflower seeds
30 ml/2 tbsp sesame seeds, lightly toasted
DRESSING:
45 ml/3 tbsp extra virgin olive oil
30 ml/2 tbsp cider vinegar
10 ml/2 tsp clear honey
juice of 1 small orange
salt and ground black pepper

1 Put the salad vegetables, raisins, almonds or cashew nuts and seeds into a large bowl.

2 Put all the dressing ingredients into a screw top jar, shake them up well and pour over the salad.

3 Toss the salad thoroughly and divide it between four small salad bowls. Season and serve lightly chilled.

Scandinavian Cucumber and Dill

It's amazing what a touch of salt can do to simple cucumber slices. They take on a contradictory soft yet crisp texture and develop a good, full flavour. However, juices continue to form after salting, so this salad is best dressed just before serving. It is particularly complementary to hot and spicy food.

SERVES 4
2 cucumbers
salt
30 ml/2 tbsp fresh chives, chopped
30 ml/2 tbsp fresh dill, chopped
150 ml/¼ pint/⅔ cup soured cream or
    fromage frais
ground black pepper

1 Slice the cucumbers as thinly as possible, preferably in a food processor or a slicer.

2 Place the slices in layers in a colander set over a plate to catch the juices. Sprinkling each layer well, but not too heavily, with salt.

3 Leave the cucumber to drain for up to 2 hours, then lay out the slices on a clean tea towel and pat them dry.

4 Mix the cucumber with the herbs, cream or fromage frais and plenty of pepper. Serve as soon as possible.

COOK'S TIP

Lightly salted (or degorged) cucumbers are also delicious as sandwich fillings in wafer thin buttered brown bread. These sandwiches were always served at the traditional British tea-time.

Spinach Roulade

A simple purée of spinach baked with eggs rolled around a creamy red pepper filling makes an exotic and colourful side dish. Even better, this can be prepared in advance and then reheated when required.

SERVES 4
450 g/1 lb leaf spinach, well washed and drained
fresh nutmeg, grated
good knob of butter
45 ml/3 tbsp Parmesan cheese, grated
45 ml/3 tbsp double cream
salt and ground black pepper
2 eggs, separated
1 small red pepper, chopped
1 × 200 g/7 oz pack soft cheese with garlic and herbs

1 Line and then grease a medium-sized Swiss roll tin. Preheat the oven to 190°C/375°F/Gas 5.

2 Cook the spinach with a tiny amount of water then drain well, pressing it through a sieve with the back of a ladle. Chop the spinach finely.

3 Mix the spinach with the nutmeg, butter, Parmesan cheese, cream and seasoning. Cool for 5 minutes then beat in the egg yolks.

4 Whisk the egg whites until they form soft peaks and carefully fold in to the spinach mixture. Spread in to the prepared tin, level and bake for 12–15 minutes until firm.

5 Turn the spinach out upside down on to a clean tea towel and allow it to cool in the tin for half an hour.

6 Meanwhile, simmer the pepper in about 30 ml/2 tbsp of water in a covered pan until just soft, then either purée it in a blender or chop it finely. Mix with the soft cheese and season well.

7 When the spinach has cooled, peel off the paper. Trim any hard edges and spread it with the red pepper cream.

8 Carefully roll up the spinach and pepper in the tea towel, leave for 10 minutes to firm up, then serve on a long platter, cut in thick slices.

VARIATION

A thick vegetable purée of any root vegetable also works well as a roulade. Try cooked beetroot or parsnip, flavouring lightly with a mild curry-style spice such as cumin or coriander. The fillings can be varied too, such as finely chopped and sautéed mushroom and onion or grated carrot mixed with fromage frais and chives. Roulades are delicious served warm as well. Sprinkle with cheese and bake in a moderately hot oven for 15 minutes or so.

Indian Spiced Okra with Almonds

Long and elegantly shaped, it's not surprising these vegetables have the popular name of 'lady's fingers'. Although commonly used in many international dishes, okra are particularly well suited to all the Indian spices.

SERVES 2–4
225 g/8 oz okra
50 g/2 oz/½ cup blanched almonds, chopped
25 g/1 oz/2 tbsp butter
15 ml/1 tbsp sunflower oil
2 garlic cloves, crushed
2.5 cm/1 in cube fresh root ginger, grated
5 ml/1 tsp cumin seeds
5 ml/1 tsp ground coriander
5 ml/1 tsp paprika

1 Trim just the tops of the okra stems and around the edges of the stalks. They have a sticky liquid which oozes out if prepared too far ahead, so trim them immediately before cooking.

2 In a shallow fireproof dish, fry the almonds in the butter until they are lightly golden, then remove.

3 Add the oil to the pan and fry the okra, stirring constantly, for 2 minutes.

4 Add the garlic and ginger and fry gently for a minute, then add the spices and cook for another minute or so, stirring all the time.

VARIATION

Okra are also popular in Louisiana cooking and are an essential ingredient for gumbo, a thick, spicy stew served over hot, steaming rice. Indeed, 'gumbo' was the old African word for okra used by the American slaves. You can make a ratatouille-style vegetable stew using okra instead of aubergines, and adding onions, peppers, garlic and tomatoes. Or try them sliced, fried in garlic and spices, then stirred into a pilaff of basmati rice with cauliflower florets and carrots. This makes a colourful and delicious dish – especially when topped with crushed grilled popadums.

5 Pour in about 300 ml/½ pint/1¼ cups water. Season well, cover and simmer for about 5 minutes or so until the okra feel just tender.

6 Finally, mix in the fried almonds and serve piping hot.

Roasted Peppers in Oil

Peppers take on a delicious, smoky flavour if roasted in a very hot oven. The skins can easily be peeled off and the flesh stored in olive oil. This oil can then be used to add extra flavour to salad dressings.

6 large peppers of differing colours
450 ml/¾ pint/scant 2 cups olive oil

1 Preheat the oven to the highest temperature, about 230°C/450°F/Gas 8. Lightly grease a large baking sheet.

2 Quarter the peppers, remove the cores and seeds then squash them flat with the back of your hands. Lay the peppers skin side up on the baking tray.

3 Roast the peppers at the top of the oven until the skins blacken and blister. This will take about 12–15 minutes.

4 Remove the peppers from the oven, cover with a clean tea towel until they are cool, then peel off the skins.

5 Slice the peppers and pack them into a clean preserving jar.

COOK'S TIP

These pepper slices make very attractive presents, especially around Christmas time. You can either buy special preserving jars from kitchen equipment shops, or wash out large jam jars, soaking off the labels at the same time. The jars should then be sterilized by placing upside down in a low oven for about half an hour. Fill the jars while still hot with the sliced peppers, and fill with a good olive oil. Cover immediately with the lid and fix on an attractive label.

6 Add the oil to the jar to completely cover the peppers, then seal the lid tightly.

7 Store the peppers in the refrigerator and use them within 2 weeks. Use the oil in dressing or for cooking once the peppers have been eaten.

Potato Latkes

These little potato pancakes make a pleasant and unusual alternative to chips or roast potatoes.

MAKES ABOUT 24
1 kg/2 lb potatoes, peeled and coarsely grated
40 g/1½ oz/scant ½ cup self-raising flour
2 eggs
15 ml/1 tbsp onion, grated
fresh nutmeg, grated
salt and ground black pepper
oil, for shallow frying

1 Soak the grated potato in plenty of cold water for about an hour, then drain well and pat dry with a clean tea towel.

2 Beat together the flour, eggs, onion and nutmeg, then mix in the potato. Season well.

3 Heat a thin layer of oil in a heavy based frying pan and drop about a tablespoon of potato batter into the pan, squashing it flat, if necessary.

4 Cook the potato until golden brown, then flip over and cook the other side. Drain on kitchen paper towel and keep warm, uncovered in the oven. Repeat with the rest of the mixture.

Stir-fry Aubergine

A speedy side dish with an Oriental touch. The aubergine is stir-fried with red pepper and black beans which gives it an exotic and colourful appearance. Salted black beans are sold either dried or canned. Dried ones will need soaking.

SERVES 4
30 ml/2 tbsp groundnut oil
1 aubergine, sliced
2 spring onions, sliced diagonally
1 garlic clove, crushed
1 small red pepper, sliced
30 ml/2 tbsp oyster sauce
25 g/1 oz/1 tbsp Chinese salted black beans, soaked if dried
ground black pepper
15 ml/1 tbsp fresh coriander or parsley, chopped, to garnish

1 Heat the oil in a wok and stir-fry the aubergine for 2 minutes. Add the onions, garlic and pepper and cook for a further 2 minutes.

2 Add the oyster sauce, black beans and pepper. Cook for a further 1 minute, season with pepper only and serve with fresh coriander or parsley.

Potato and Parsnip Dauphinoise

Layers of potatoes and parsnips are baked slowly in creamy milk with grated cheese. This is an ideal special side dish or light supper dish.

SERVES 4–6
1 kg/2 lb potatoes, thinly sliced
1 onion, thinly sliced
450 g/1 lb parsnips, thinly sliced
2 garlic cloves, crushed
50 g/2 oz/4 tbsp butter
125 g/4 oz Gruyère or Cheddar cheese, grated
fresh nutmeg, grated
salt and ground black pepper
300 ml/½ pint/1¼ cups single cream
300 ml/½ pint/1¼ cups milk

1 Lightly grease a large shallow ovenproof dish. Preheat the oven to 180°C/350°F/Gas 4.

2 Layer the potatoes with the onion and parsnips. In between each layer, dot the vegetables with garlic and butter, sprinkle over most of the cheese, add the nutmeg and season well.

3 Heat the cream and milk together in a saucepan until it is hot but not boiling. Slowly pour the creamy milk over the vegetables, making sure it seeps underneath them.

4 Scatter the remaining cheese over the vegetables and grate a little more nutmeg on top. Bake for about an hour or so until the potatoes are tender and the cheesey top is bubbling and golden.

Asparagus Mimosa

Pretty spears of fresh, tender asparagus are tossed in a buttery sauce and served with a chopped egg and chervil dressing. This also makes an excellent starter.

SERVES 2
225 g/8 oz fresh asparagus
salt
ground black pepper
50 g/2 oz/4 tbsp butter, melted
squeeze of fresh lemon juice
2 eggs, hard-boiled and chopped
15 ml/1 tbsp fresh chervil, chopped

1 Trim the asparagus stalks and peel off the tough outer layers at the base with a vegetable peeler.

2 Poach the asparagus spears in lightly salted water, until just tender. This will take between 3–6 minutes. (Use a clean, deep frying pan if you don't have an asparagus steamer.)

3 Drain the asparagus well and arrange it on two small plates or one large one. Season well.

4 Mix the melted butter with the lemon juice. Trickle over the spears, sprinkle with the eggs and garnish with the chervil. Serve warm.

Braised Fennel and Tomato

Fennel is a very undervalued vegetable but it is excellent cooked in a light tomato sauce. This dish can be gently simmered on the cooker or baked inside a moderate oven.

SERVES 4–6
2 fennel bulbs
1 small onion or 3 shallots, sliced
1 garlic clove, crushed
30 ml/2 tbsp olive oil
4 medium sized tomatoes, skinned and chopped
45 ml/3 tbsp dry white wine
15 ml/1 tbsp fresh marjoram, chopped
150 ml/¼ pint/⅔ cup stock or water
salt and ground black pepper

1 Trim the fennel then cut it into wedges. Reserve any fronds for a garnish.

2 Lightly sauté the fennel with the onion or shallots and garlic in the oil in a fireproof dish for 5 minutes.

3 Add the tomatoes, wine, marjoram and stock or water. Season.

4 Cover and either simmer very gently for 20 minutes, or bake in a preheated oven for 30 minutes at 190°C/375°F/Gas 5. Garnish with any reserved fronds and serve immediately.

Creamed Winter Vegetables

A mixture of chunky mashed root vegetables, such as carrots, parsnips and turnips or swedes, makes a wonderfully warming winter side dish.

SERVES 4–6
225 g/8 oz carrots, chopped
225 g/8 oz parsnips, chopped
1 small swede, chopped
25 g/1 oz/2 tbsp butter
10 ml/2 tsp mild curry paste
salt and ground black pepper
115 g/4 oz/½ cup fromage frais
15 ml/1 tbsp fresh chives, chopped

1 Boil the carrots, parsnips and swede in plenty of lightly salted water until tender. Drain the vegetables then return them to the pan with the butter, curry paste and seasoning.

2 Mash the vegetables lightly with a fork so that you end up with a chunky purée; you want to retain a good texture.

3 Stir in the fromage frais and chives. Check the seasoning and serve hot. This is a good dish to prepare in advance and reheat when required.

COOK'S TIP

Vegetable purées are a popular accompaniment with any dish which could be a little on the dry side, providing a good contrast of textures and colours. Suitable vegetables are Brussels sprouts, carrots, peas, broccoli and leeks.

PARTIES & PICNICS

From informal meals, ideal for outdoor entertaining, to elegant and delicious dishes that will add style to special occasions, here are recipes to suit every festivity.

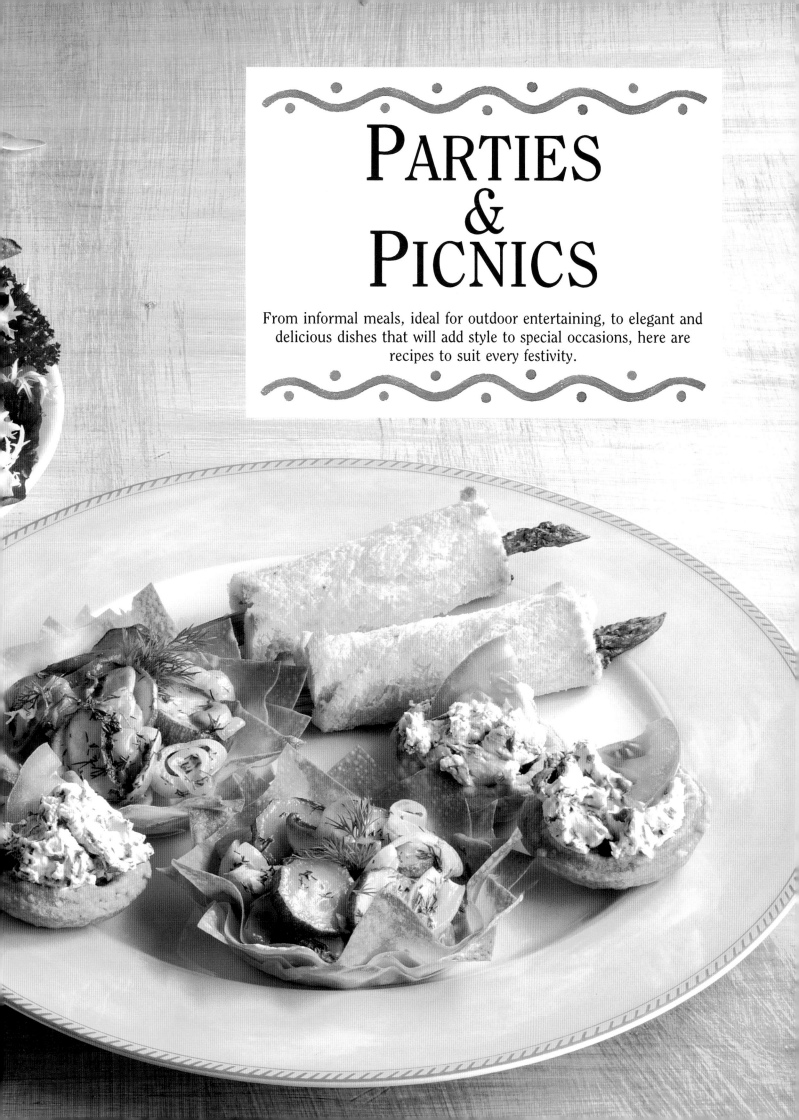

Spicy Potato Strudel

Wrap up a tasty mixture of vegetables in a spicy, creamy sauce with crisp filo pastry. It makes a perfect dish for a special family supper.

SERVES 4
1 onion, chopped
2 carrots, coarsely grated
1 courgette, chopped
350 g/12 oz potatoes, chopped
65 g/2½ oz/5 tbsp butter
10 ml/2 tsp mild curry paste
2.5 ml/½ tsp dried thyme
150 ml/¼ pint/⅔ cup water
salt and ground black pepper
1 egg, beaten
30 ml/2 tbsp single cream
50 g/2 oz Cheddar cheese, grated
8 sheets filo pastry
sesame seeds, to sprinkle

1 Fry the onion, carrots, courgette and potatoes in half the butter for 5 minutes until they are soft then add the curry paste and cook for a further minute.

2 Add the thyme, water and seasoning. Continue to cook gently, uncovered for another 10 minutes.

3 Allow the mixture to cool and mix in the egg, cream and cheese. Chill until ready to fill and roll.

4 Melt the remaining butter and lay out four sheets of filo pastry, slightly overlapping them to form a large rectangle. Brush with butter and fit the other sheets on top. Brush again.

5 Spoon the filling along one long edge, then roll up the pastry. Form it into a circle and brush again with the last of the butter. Sprinkle over the sesame seeds and set on a baking sheet.

6 Heat the oven to 190°C/375°F/Gas 5 then bake the strudel for about 25 minutes until golden and crisp. Allow to stand for 5 minutes or so before cutting.

Coronation Salad

This famous salad dressing was created especially for the coronation dinner of Queen Elizabeth II. It is a wonderful accompaniment to eggs and vegetables.

SERVES 6
450 g/1 lb new potatoes
salt
45 ml/3 tbsp vinaigrette dressing
3 spring onions, chopped
ground black pepper
6 eggs, hard-boiled and halved
frilly lettuce leaves, to serve
¼ cucumber, sliced then cut in shreds
6 large radishes, sliced
carton of salad cress
DRESSING
30 ml/2 tbsp olive oil
1 small onion, chopped
15 ml/1 tbsp mild curry
   powder or korma spice mix
10 ml/2 tsp tomato purée
30 ml/2 tbsp lemon juice
30 ml/2 tbsp sherry
300 ml/½ pint/1¼ cups mayonnaise
150 ml/¼ pint/¾ cup natural yogurt

1 Boil the potatoes in salted water until tender. Drain them and toss in the vinaigrette dressing.

2 Allow the potatoes to cool, stirring in the spring onions and seasoning. Cool the mixture thoroughly.

3 Meanwhile, make the coronation dressing. Heat the oil and fry the onion for 3 minutes until it is soft. Stir in the spice powder and fry for a further minute. Mix in all the other dressing ingredients.

4 Stir the dressing into the potatoes; add the eggs then chill. Line a serving platter with lettuce leaves and pile the salad in the centre. Scatter over the cucumber, radishes and cress.

Pasta and Wild Mushroom Mould

Bake pasta shapes in a golden crumb coating layered with a rich bechamel sauce and mushrooms. Scrumptious!

SERVES 4–6
200 g/7 oz pasta shapes
600 ml/1 pint/2½ cups milk
1 bay leaf
small onion stuck with 6 cloves
50 g/2 oz/4 tbsp butter
45 ml/3 tbsp breadcrumbs
10 ml/2 tsp dried mixed herbs
40 g/1½ oz/⅓ cup plain flour
60 ml/4 tbsp Parmesan cheese, freshly grated
fresh nutmeg, grated
salt and ground black pepper
2 eggs, beaten
1 × 15 g/½ oz pack porcini dried mushrooms
350 g/12 oz button mushrooms, sliced
2 garlic cloves, crushed
30 ml/2 tbsp olive oil
30 ml/ 2 tbsp fresh parsley, chopped

1 Boil the pasta according to the instructions on the pack. Drain and set aside. Heat the milk with the bay leaf and clove-studded onion and stand for 15 minutes. Remove bay leaf and onion.

2 Melt the butter in a saucepan and use a little to brush the inside of a large oval pie dish. Mix the crumbs and mixed herbs together and use them to coat the inside of the dish.

3 Stir the flour into the butter, cook for a minute then slowly add the hot milk to make a smooth sauce. Add the cheese, nutmeg, seasoning and cooked pasta. Cool for 5 minutes then beat in the eggs.

4 Soak the porcini in a little hot water until they are soft. Reserve the liquor and chop the porcini.

5 Fry the porcini with the sliced mushrooms and garlic in the olive oil for about 3 minutes. Season well, stir in the liquor and reduce down. Add the parsley.

6 Spoon a layer of pasta in the dish. Sprinkle over the mushrooms then more pasta and so on, finishing with pasta. Cover with greased foil. Heat the oven to 190°C/375°F/Gas 5 and bake for about 25–30 minutes. Allow to stand for 5 minutes before turning out to serve.

Aubergine Boats

These can be prepared ahead and baked prior to eating. The hazelnut topping contrasts nicely with the smooth aubergine filling.

SERVES 4
115 g/4 oz/⅔ cup brown basmati rice
2 medium size aubergines, halved lengthways
1 onion, chopped
2 garlic cloves, crushed
1 small green pepper, chopped
115 g/4 oz mushrooms, sliced
45 ml/3 tbsp olive oil
75 g/3 oz Cheddar cheese, grated
1 egg, beaten
2.5 ml/½ tsp marjoram
salt and ground black pepper
30 ml/2 tbsp hazelnuts, chopped

1 Boil the rice according to the instructions on the pack, drain and then cool. Scoop out the flesh from the aubergines and chop. Blanch the shells in boiling water for 2 minutes then drain upside down.

2 Fry the aubergine flesh, onion, garlic, pepper and mushrooms in the oil, for about 5 minutes.

3 Mix in the rice, cheese, egg, marjoram and seasoning. Arrange the aubergine shells in an ovenproof dish. Spoon the filling inside. Sprinkle over the nuts. Chill until ready to bake.

4 Heat the oven to 190°C/375°F/Gas 5 and bake the aubergines for about 25 minutes until the filling is set and the nuts are golden brown.

Crêpe Galette

Make a stack of light pancakes and layer them together with a tasty lentil filling for an impressive dinner party main course. Serve with a homemade tomato sauce.

SERVES 6
115 g/4 oz/1 cup plain flour
good pinch of salt
1 egg
300 ml/½ pint/1¼ cups buttermilk, or milk and water, mixed
oil, for cooking
FILLING
2 leeks, thinly sliced
1 small fennel bulb, thinly sliced
60 ml/4 tbsp olive oil
150 g/6 oz/¾ cup red lentils
150 ml/¼ pint/⅔ cup dry white wine
1 × 400 g/14 oz can chopped tomatoes
300 ml/½ pint/1¼ cups stock
5 ml/1 tsp dried oregano
salt and ground black pepper
1 onion, sliced
225 g/8 oz mushrooms, sliced
225 g/8 oz frozen leaf spinach, thawed and squeezed dry
200 g/7 oz low fat cream cheese
50 g/2 oz Parmesan cheese, freshly grated

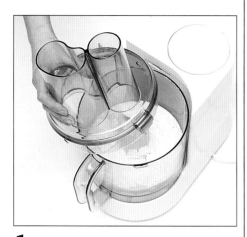

1 Make the pancake batter by mixing the flour, salt, egg and buttermilk or milk and water in a blender until smooth. Set aside while you prepare the filling.

2 Gently fry the leeks and fennel in half the olive oil for 5 minutes, then add the lentils and wine. Cook for a minute until reduced down then stir in the tomatoes and stock.

3 Bring the leek/fennel mixture to a boil, add the oregano and seasoning then simmer for 20 minutes, stirring it occasionally until it thickens.

4 Fry the onion and mushrooms in the remaining olive oil for 5 minutes, stir in the spinach and heat. Season well then mix in the cream cheese.

5 Make about 12–14 pancakes with the batter in a well heated non-stick frying pan. Lightly grease a 20 cm/8 in round deep spring-form cake tin and line the base and sides with some of the pancakes, overlapping them as necessary.

6 Layer the remaining pancakes with the two fillings, sprinkling Parmesan in between and pressing them down well. Finish with a pancake on top.

7 Cover with foil and set aside to rest. Preheat the oven to 190°C/375°F/Gas 5. Bake for about 40 minutes, then turn out and allow to firm up for 10 minutes before cutting into wedges.

COOK'S TIP

This can be frozen ready made up, but it is probably nicer if frozen in parts – the pancakes interleaved with greaseproof paper and then wrapped in foil and the sauce frozen separately.

Polenta Fingers with Beans and Tomatoes

Polenta, or cornmeal, is a popular family favourite in Italy. It is eaten either hot from a bowl or allowed to set, cut into fingers, and grilled.

SERVES 6
1.75 litres/3 pints/7½ cups milk and water, mixed
10 ml/2 tsp salt
275 g/10 oz/1½ cups polenta
25 g/1 oz/2 tbsp butter, plus extra for spreading
50 g/2 oz Parmesan cheese, freshly grated
ground black pepper
SAUCE
1 onion, chopped
2 garlic cloves, crushed
30 ml/2 tbsp olive oil
1 × 400 g/14 oz can chopped tomatoes
salt and ground black pepper
good pinch of dried sage
225 g/8 oz frozen broad beans

1 In a large saucepan, bring the milk and water to a boil. Stir in the salt. While stirring with a wooden spoon trickle the polenta into the boiling liquid in a steady stream and continue stirring until the mixture has thickened.

2 Lower the heat and simmer for about 20 minutes, stirring frequently. Add the butter, cheese and seasoning.

3 Lightly grease a shallow roasting pan and pour in the polenta mixture. Cool, then chill overnight.

4 For the sauce, fry the onion and garlic in the oil for 5 minutes. Add the tomatoes, seasoning and sage and cook for a further 10 minutes. Stir in the broad beans and cook for 5 minutes more.

5 Turn out the polenta and cut into fingers. Grill both sides until brown and crisp. Spread with a little butter and serve accompanied by the tomato and beans.

Paprika and Parmesan Tartlets

Pretty pink pastry tarts with a tangy cream filling are ideal for handing round at drinks parties. Make the cases ahead of the party and fill them just before serving.

MAKES 18
225 g/8 oz/2 cups plain flour
10 ml/2 tsp paprika
150 g/5 oz/10 tbsp butter or sunflower margarine
40 g/1½ oz Parmesan cheese, freshly grated
cold water, to bind
FILLING
350 g/12 oz goats' cheese
50 g/2 oz rocket leaves, or watercress, chopped
30 ml/2 tbsp fresh chives, chopped
salt and ground black pepper
450 g/1 lb tomatoes, sliced

1 Sift the flour with the paprika and rub in the butter or margarine. Stir in the Parmesan and mix to a firm dough with cold water.

2 Roll out the pastry and stamp out 18 rounds, large enough to fit into bun tins. Prick the bases well with a fork and chill while you preheat the oven to 190°C/375°F/Gas 5.

3 Bake the tartlets for 15 minutes until crisp. Cool them on a wire rack.

4 Beat the cheese with the rocket or cress, chives and seasoning. Slice the tomatoes, allowing roughly two slices per tart.

5 When ready to serve, spoon the filling into the tarts. Top each one with some tomato and garnish with extra rocket or cress leaves.

Basmati and Blue Lentil Salad 🌿

Puy lentils from France (sometimes known as blue lentils) are small, deliciously nutty pulses, highly prized by gourmets. They blend beautifully with aromatic basmati rice.

SERVES 6
115 g/4 oz/⅔ cup puys de dome lentils, soaked
225 g/8 oz/1¼ cups basmati rice, rinsed well
2 carrots, coarsely grated
⅓ cucumber, halved, seeded and coarsely grated
3 spring onions, sliced
45 ml/3 tbsp fresh parsley, chopped
DRESSING
30 ml/2 tbsp sunflower oil
30 ml/2 tbsp extra virgin olive oil
30 ml/2 tbsp wine vinegar
30 ml/2 tbsp fresh lemon juice
good pinch of granulated sugar
salt and ground black pepper

1 Soak the lentils for 30 minutes. Meanwhile, make the dressing by shaking all the ingredients together in a screw-topped jar. Set aside.

2 Boil the lentils in plenty of unsalted water for 20–25 minutes or until soft. Drain thoroughly.

3 Boil the basmati rice for 10 minutes, then drain.

4 Mix together the rice and lentils in the dressing and season well. Leave to cool.

5 Add the carrots, cucumber, onions and parsley. Spoon into an attractive serving bowl and chill before serving.

Wild Rice with Julienne Vegetables

Make an accompanying dish more interesting with some exquisite wild rice. For the best flavour, buy a good quality wild rice (which is actually a cereal!) and, to shorten the cooking time, soak it overnight.

SERVES 4
115 g/4 oz/½ cup wild rice
1 red onion, sliced
2 carrots, cut in julienne sticks
2 celery sticks, cut in julienne sticks
50 g/2 oz/4 tbsp butter
150 ml/¼ pint/⅔ cup stock or water
salt and ground black pepper
2 medium courgettes, cut in thicker sticks
a few toasted almond flakes, to serve

1 Drain the soaked rice, then boil in plenty of unsalted water for 15–20 minutes, until it is soft and many of the grains have burst open. Drain.

2 In another saucepan, gently fry the onion, carrots and celery in the butter for 2 minutes then pour in the stock or water and season well.

3 Bring to a boil, simmer for 2 minutes then stir in the courgettes. Cook for 1 more minute then mix in the rice. Reheat and serve hot sprinkled with the almonds.

Oven-Crisp Asparagus Rolls

A lovely treat when fresh asparagus is in season is to wrap blanched spears in slices of thin bread and bake in a buttery glaze until crisp. Out of season, use canned or frozen spears.

SERVES 8
8 thick spears of fresh asparagus
salt
115 g/4 oz/8½ tbsp butter, softened
15 ml/1 tbsp coarse grained mustard
grated rind of 1 lemon
ground black pepper
8 slices thin white bread, crusts removed

1 Trim the asparagus stalks, peeling the tough woody skin at the base. Blanch until just tender in a shallow pan of boiling, salted water. Drain and refresh in cold water. Pat dry.

2 Blend two-thirds of the butter with the mustard, lemon rind and seasoning. Spread over the slices of bread.

3 Lay an asparagus spear on the edge of each bread slice and roll it up tightly. Place the rolls join side down on a lightly greased baking sheet.

4 Melt the remaining butter and brush over the rolls. Heat the oven to 190°C/375°F/Gas 5 and bake for 12–15 minutes until golden and crisp. Cool slightly before serving.

VARIATION

Asparagus has always been something of a luxury as its season is so short, but imports from across the world mean that it is available almost all year round, albeit at a price!

Thin baby asparagus, known as sprue, can be eaten raw in salads or stir-fried quickly. Opinions differ about the merits of green or white asparagus spears. The latter are forced in the dark (hence their white colour), but some people consider them to have a better flavour and texture.

Ratatouille Tart

Serve this pretty tart warm so the cheese is easy to cut and eat. For the best results, make the base and filling separately then heat and combine just before serving.

SERVES 6
115 g/4 oz/1 cup plain flour
115 g/4 oz/¾ cup wholemeal flour
5 ml/1 tsp dried mixed herbs
salt and ground black pepper
115 g/4 oz/½ cup sunflower margarine
45–60 ml/3–4 tbsp cold water
FILLING
1 small aubergine, thickly sliced
salt
45 ml/3 tbsp olive oil
1 onion, sliced
1 red or yellow pepper, sliced
2 garlic cloves, crushed
2 courgettes, thickly sliced
2 tomatoes, skinned and sliced
ground black pepper
30 ml/2 tbsp fresh basil, chopped
150 g/5 oz Mozzarella cheese, sliced
30 ml/2 tbsp pine nuts

1 Mix the two flours with the herbs and seasoning then rub in the margarine until it resembles fine crumbs. Mix to a firm dough with water.

2 Roll out the pastry and line a 23 cm/ 9 in round flan tin. Prick the base, line with foil and baking beans then allow to rest in the fridge.

3 Meanwhile, sprinkle the aubergine lightly with salt and leave to drain for 30 minutes in a colander. Rinse and pat dry.

4 Heat the oil in a frying pan and fry the onion and pepper for 5 minutes, then add the garlic, courgettes and aubergine. Fry for a further 10 minutes, stirring the mixture occasionally.

5 Stir in the tomatoes and seasoning, cook for a further 3 minutes, add the basil then remove the pan from the heat and allow to cool.

6 Heat the oven to 200°C/400°F/Gas 6. Place the flan on a baking sheet and bake for 25 minutes, removing the foil and baking beans for the last 5 minutes. Cool and then, if possible, remove the case from the tin.

7 When ready to serve, spoon the vegetables into the case using a slotted spoon so any juices drain off and don't soak into the pastry. Top with the cheese slices and pine nuts. Toast under a preheated grill until golden and bubbling. Serve warm.

Filo Baskets with Ginger Dill Vegetables

Make up some elegant filo baskets, then fill with some crisply steamed vegetables tossed in an interesting and tasty sauce.

SERVES 4
4 sheets of filo pastry
40 g/1½ oz/3 tbsp butter, melted
FILLING
30 ml/2 tbsp olive oil
15 ml/1 tbsp fresh root ginger, grated
2 garlic cloves, crushed
3 shallots, sliced
225 g/8 oz mushrooms, chestnut or
    brown, sliced
115 g/4 oz oyster mushrooms, sliced
1 courgette, sliced
200 g/7 oz crème fraîche
30 ml/2 tbsp fresh dill, chopped
salt and ground black pepper
dill and parsley sprigs, to serve

1 Cut the filo sheets into four. Line four Yorkshire pudding tins, angling the layers so that the corners form a pretty star shape. Brush between each layer with butter. Set aside.

2 Heat the oven to 190°C/375°F/Gas 5. Bake the cases for about 10 minutes until golden brown and crisp. Remove and cool.

3 For the filling, heat the oil and sauté the ginger, garlic and shallots for 2 minutes, then add the mushrooms and courgette. Cook for another 3 minutes.

4 Mix in the crème fraîche, chopped dill and seasoning. Heat until just bubbling then spoon into the filo cases. Garnish with the dill and parsley and serve.

Gado Gado Salad with Peanut Sambal

Indonesians enjoy a salad of lightly-steamed vegetables topped with a peanut sauce. It is ideal for a colourful summer buffet dish.

SERVES 6
225 g/8 oz new potatoes, halved
2 carrots, cut in sticks
115 g/4 oz green beans
½ small cauliflower, broken into florets
¼ firm white cabbage, shredded
200 g/7 oz bean or lentil sprouts
4 eggs, hard-boiled and quartered
bunch watercress, trimmed
SAUCE
90 ml/6 tbsp crunchy peanut butter
300 ml/½ pint/1¼ cups cold water
1 garlic clove, crushed
30 ml/2 tbsp dark soy sauce
15 ml/1 tbsp dry sherry
10 ml/2 tsp caster sugar
15 ml/1 tbsp fresh lemon juice
5 ml/1 tsp anchovy essence

1 Fit a steamer or metal colander over a pan of gently boiling water. Cook the potatoes for 10 minutes.

2 Add the rest of the vegetables and sprouts and steam for a further 10 minutes until tender. Cool and serve on a platter with the egg quarters surrounded by the watercress.

3 Beat all the sauce ingredients together until smooth. Put the sauce in a small bowl and drizzle over each individual serving of salad.

Vegetable Fritters with Tzatziki

Spicy deep-fried aubergine and courgette slices served with a creamy Greek yogurt and dill dip make a good, simple party starter or an excellent side dish.

SERVES 4–6
½ cucumber, coarsely grated
225 g/8 oz Greek natural yogurt
15 ml/1 tbsp extra virgin olive oil
10 ml/2 tsp fresh lemon juice
30 ml/2 tbsp fresh dill, chopped
15 ml/1 tbsp fresh mint, chopped
1 garlic clove, crushed
salt and ground black pepper
1 large aubergine, thickly sliced
2 courgettes, thickly sliced
1 egg white, beaten
40 g/1½ oz/4 tbsp plain flour
10 ml/2 tsp ground coriander
ground cumin

1 For the dip, mix the cucumber, yogurt, oil, lemon juice, dill, mint, garlic and seasoning. Spoon into a bowl then set aside.

2 Layer the aubergine and courgettes in a colander and sprinkle them with salt. Leave for 30 minutes. Rinse in cold water then pat dry.

3 Put the egg white into a bowl. Mix the flour, coriander and cumin with seasoning and put into another bowl.

4 Dip the vegetables first into the egg white then into the seasoned flour and set aside.

5 Heat about 2.5 cm/1 in of oil in a deep frying pan until quite hot, then fry the vegetables a few at a time until they are golden and crisp.

6 Drain and keep warm while you fry the remainder. Serve warm on a platter with a bowl of the tzatziki dip lightly sprinkled with paprika.

Mushroom Saucers

Recipes which are already portioned are a great boon for the host, as guests can help themselves without feeling they are taking more than their fair share. Large flat mushrooms are great for this reason.

SERVES 8
8 large flat mushrooms with stalks removed, wiped clean and chopped
45 ml/3 tbsp olive oil
salt and ground black pepper
1 onion, sliced
5 ml/1 tsp cumin seeds
450 g/1 lb leaf spinach, stalks trimmed, and shredded
1 × 425 g/15 oz can red kidney beans, drained
1 × 200 g/7 oz pack soft cheese with garlic and herbs
2 medium tomatoes, halved, seeded and sliced in strips

1 Heat the oven to 190°C/375°F/Gas 5. Lightly grease a large, shallow ovenproof dish. Brush the mushrooms with some oil, place them in the dish and season well. Cover with foil and bake for 15–20 minutes. Uncover, drain and reserve the juices.

3 Stir in the spinach and fry until the leaves begin to wilt, then mix in the beans and heat well. Add the cheese, stirring until melted and season again.

4 Divide the mixture between the mushroom cups and return to the oven to heat through. Serve garnished with tomato slices.

2 Fry the onion and chopped mushroom stalks in the remaining oil for 5 minutes until soft. Then add the cumin seeds and mushroom juices and cook for a minute longer until reduced down.

Marbled Quails' Eggs

Hard-boiled quails' eggs re-boiled in smoky China tea assume a pretty marbled skin. It's quite a treat to dip them into a fragrant spicy salt and hand them round with drinks. Szechuan peppercorns can be bought from Oriental food stores.

SERVES 4–6
12 quails' eggs
600 ml/1 pint/2½ cups strong lapsang souchong tea
15 ml/1 tbsp dark soy sauce
15 ml/1 tbsp dry sherry
2 star anise pods
lettuce leaves, to serve
milled Szechuan red peppercorns
sea salt, to mix

1 Place the quails' eggs in cold water and bring to the boil. Time them for 2 minutes from when the water boils.

2 Remove the eggs from the pan and run them under cold water to cool. Tap the shells all over so they are crazed, but do not peel yet.

3 In a saucepan, bring the tea to the boil and add the soy sauce, sherry and star anise. Re-boil the eggs for about 15 minutes, partially covered, so the liquid does not boil dry.

4 Cool the eggs, then peel them and arrange on a small platter lined with lettuce leaves. Mix the ground red peppercorns with equal quantities of salt and place in a small side dish.

Beetroot Roulade

This roulade is simple to make, yet will create a stunning impression. Prepare it in the autumn when beetroots are at their best.

SERVES 6
225 g/8 oz fresh beetroot, cooked and peeled
2.5 ml/½ tsp ground cumin
25 g/1 oz/2 tbsp butter
10 ml/2 tsp grated onion
4 eggs, separated
salt and ground black pepper
FILLING
150 ml/¼ pint/⅔ cup crème frâiche or double cream
10 ml/2 tsp white wine vinegar
good pinch dry mustard powder
5 ml/1 tsp sugar
45 ml/3 tbsp fresh parsley, chopped
30 ml/2 tbsp fresh dill, chopped
45 ml/3 tbsp horseradish relish

1 Line and grease a Swiss roll tin. Preheat the oven to 190°C/375°F/Gas 5.

2 Roughly chop the beetroot then blend to a purée in a food processor and beat in the cumin, butter, onion, egg yolks and seasoning. Turn the beetroot purée into a large bowl.

3 In another bowl, that is spotlessly clean, whisk the egg whites until they form soft peaks. Fold them into the beetroot mixture carefully.

4 Spoon the mixture into the Swiss roll tin, level and bake for about 15 minutes until just firm to touch.

5 Have ready a clean tea towel laid over a wire rack. Turn the beetroot out onto the towel, and remove the paper carefully in strips.

6 Beat the crème frâiche or cream until lightly stiff, then fold in the remaining ingredients. Spread this mixture onto the beetroot. Roll up the roulade in the towel and allow it to cool.

Pasta and Beetroot Salad

Colour is vital at a party table, and this salad is certainly eye catching. Serve the egg and avocado at the last moment to avoid discoloration.

SERVES 8
2 uncooked beetroots, scrubbed
225 g/8 oz pasta shells or twists
45 ml/3 tbsp vinaigrette dressing
salt and ground black pepper
2 celery sticks, thinly sliced
3 spring onions, sliced
75 g/3 oz/²⁄₃ cup walnuts or hazelnuts, roughly chopped
1 dessert apple, cored, halved and sliced
DRESSING
60 ml/4 tbsp mayonnaise
45 ml/3 tbsp natural yogurt or fromage frais
30 ml/2 tbsp milk
10 ml/2 tsp horseradish relish
TO SERVE
curly lettuce leaves
3 eggs, hard boiled and chopped
2 ripe avocadoes
box of salad cress

1 Boil the beetroots, without peeling them, in lightly salted water until they are just tender. Drain, cool, peel and chop. Set aside.

2 Cook the pasta according to the instructions on the pack then drain and toss in the vinaigrette and season well. Cool. Mix the pasta with the beetroot, celery, onions, nuts and apple.

3 Stir all the dressing ingredients together and mix into the pasta bowl. Chill well.

4 To serve, line a pretty salad bowl with the lettuce leaves and pile the salad in the centre. When ready to serve, scatter over the chopped egg. Peel and slice the avocadoes and arrange them on top then sprinkle over the cress.

Gazpacho

This classic Spanish no-cook soup is ideal for taking on picnics as it can be packed straight from the refrigerator. Keep the chopped vegetables in separate pots and hand them round as an accompaniment.

SERVES 6
1 slice white bread, crusts removed
cold water, to soak
1 garlic clove, crushed
30 ml/2 tbsp extra virgin olive oil
30 ml/2 tbsp white wine vinegar
6 large ripe tomatoes, skinned and finely chopped
1 small onion, finely chopped
2.5 ml/½ tsp paprika
good pinch ground cumin
150 ml/¼ pint/²⁄₃ cup tomato juice
salt and ground black pepper
TO GARNISH
1 green pepper, chopped
⅓ cucumber, peeled, seeded and chopped
CROÛTONS
2 slices bread, cubed and deep fried

1 Soak the bread slice in enough cold water just to cover and leave for about 5 minutes, then mash with a fork.

2 Pound the garlic, oil and vinegar with a pestle and mortar or blend in a food processor. Mix this into the bread.

3 Spoon the mixture into a bowl and stir in the tomatoes, onion, spices and tomato juice. Season well and store in the refrigerator. Prepare the garnishes and store these in separate containers.

4 For a picnic, pour the chilled soup into a flask. Otherwise, pour into a chilled glass salad bowl and hand the garnishes round in smaller bowls.

Sesame Egg Roll

A Japanese-inspired idea. An egg pancake is rolled up with a creamy watercress filling and served cut in thick slices.

SERVES 3–4
3 eggs
15 ml/1 tbsp soy sauce
15 ml/1 tbsp sesame seeds
5 ml/1 tsp sesame seed oil
salt and ground black pepper
15 ml/1 tbsp sunflower oil
75 g/3 oz cream cheese with garlic
1 bunch watercress, chopped

1 Beat the eggs with the soy sauce, sesame seeds, sesame seed oil and seasoning.

2 Heat the sunflower oil in a large frying pan until quite hot, then pour in the egg mixture, tilting the pan so it covers the whole base. Cook until firm.

3 Allow the pancake to stand in the pan for a few minutes then turn out onto a chopping board and cool completely.

4 Beat the cream cheese until soft, season well then mix in the chopped watercress. Spread this over the egg pancake then roll it up quite firmly. Wrap in cling film and chill.

Homemade Coleslaw

Forget shop-bought coleslaw! Making your own at home is quite quick and easy to do – and it tastes fresh, crunchy and wonderful.

SERVES 4–6
¼ firm white cabbage
1 small onion, finely chopped
2 celery sticks, thinly sliced
2 carrots, coarsely grated
5–10 ml/1–2 tsp caraway seeds (optional)
1 dessert apple, cored and chopped
  (optional)
50 g/2 oz/½ cup walnuts, chopped
  (optional)
salt and ground black pepper
DRESSING
45 ml/3 tbsp mayonnaise
30 ml/2 tbsp single cream or natural
  yogurt
5 ml/1 tsp lemon rind, grated
salt and ground black pepper

1 Cut and discard the core from the cabbage quarter then shred the leaves finely. Place this in a large bowl.

2 Into the cabbage, toss the onion, celery and carrot, plus the caraway seeds, apple and walnuts, if using. Season well.

3 Mix the dressing ingredients together and stir into the vegetables. Cover and allow to stand for 2 hours, stirring occasionally, then chill the coleslaw lightly before serving.

Malfatti with Red Sauce

If you ever felt dumplings were a little heavy, try making these light Italian spinach and ricotta malfatti instead. Serve them with a simple tomato and red pepper sauce.

SERVES 4–6
450 g/1 lb fresh leaf spinach, stalks trimmed
1 small onion, chopped
1 garlic clove, crushed
15 ml/1 tbsp olive oil
400 g/14 oz ricotta cheese
75 g/3 oz/⅔ cup dried breadcrumbs
50 g/2 oz/½ cup plain flour
5 ml/1 tsp salt
50 g/2 oz Parmesan cheese, freshly grated
fresh nutmeg, grated, to taste
3 eggs, beaten
25 g/1 oz/2 tbsp butter, melted
SAUCE
1 large, red pepper, chopped
1 small red onion, chopped
30 ml/2 tbsp olive oil
1 × 400 g/14 oz can chopped tomatoes
150 ml/¼ pint/⅔ cup water
good pinch dried oregano
salt and ground black pepper
30 ml/2 tbsp single cream

1 Blanch the spinach in the tiniest amount of water until it is limp, then drain well, pressing it through a sieve with the back of a ladle or spoon. Chop very finely.

COOK'S TIP

Quenelles are oval-shaped dumplings. To shape the Malfatti into quenelles you need two dessertspoons. Scoop up the mixture with one spoon, making sure it is mounded up, then, using the other spoon, scoop the mixture off the first spoon, twisting the top spoon into the bowl of the second.

Repeat this action two or three times until the quenelle is smooth, and then gently knock it off onto a plate ready to cook.

2 Lightly fry the onion and garlic in the oil for 5 minutes then mix with the spinach together with the ricotta, breadcrumbs, flour, salt, most of the Parmesan and nutmeg.

3 Allow the mixture to cool, add the eggs and melted butter, then mould into 12 small 'sausage' shapes.

4 Meanwhile, make the sauce by lightly sautéeing the pepper and onion in the oil for 5 minutes. Add the tomatoes, water, oregano and seasoning. Bring to a boil, then simmer for 5 minutes.

5 When cooked, remove from the heat and blend to a purée in a food processor. Return to the pan, then stir in the cream. Check the seasoning.

6 Bring a shallow pan of salted water to a gentle boil and drop the malfatti into it a few at a time and poach them for about 5 minutes. Drain them well and keep them warm.

7 Arrange the malfatti on warm plates and drizzle over the sauce. Serve topped with the remaining Parmesan.

Curried Mango Chutney Dip

A quickly made, tangy and spicy dip or dressing, ideal as a dip for strips of pitta bread, grissini or sticks of fresh chopped vegetables.

SERVES 4–6
1 onion, chopped
1 garlic clove, crushed
30 ml/2 tbsp sunflower oil
10 ml/2 tsp mild curry powder
225 g/8 oz natural Greek yogurt
30 ml/2 tbsp mango chutney
salt and ground black pepper
30 ml/2 tbsp fresh parsley, chopped

1 Gently fry the onion and garlic in the oil for 5 minutes until they are soft. Add the curry powder and cook for a further minute then allow the mixture to cool.

2 Spoon into a food processor with the yogurt, chutney and seasoning and blend until smooth.

3 Stir in the parsley and chill before serving with a variety of vegetable crudités and strips of bread.

Nutty Mushroom Paté

Spread this delicious, medium-texture paté on chunks of crusty French bread and eat with crisp leaves of lettuce and sweet cherry tomatoes.

SERVES 4–6
1 onion, chopped
1 garlic clove, crushed
15 ml/1 tbsp sunflower oil
30 ml/2 tbsp water
15 ml/1 tbsp dry sherry
225 g/8 oz button mushrooms, chopped
salt and ground black pepper
75 g/3 oz/¾ cup cashew nuts or walnuts, chopped
150 g/5 oz low fat soft cheese
15 ml/1 tbsp soy sauce
few dashes Worcestershire sauce
fresh parsley, chopped, and a little paprika, to serve

1 Gently fry the onion and garlic in the oil for 3 minutes then add the water, sherry and mushrooms. Cook, stirring for about 5 minutes. Season to taste and allow to cool a little.

2 Put the mixture into a food processor with the nuts, cheese and sauces. Blend to a rough purée – do not allow it to become too smooth.

3 Check the seasoning then spoon into a serving dish. Swirl the top and serve lightly chilled sprinkled with parsley and paprika.

Antipasti with Aioli

For a simple starter or hand-around cocktail canapé, make a bowl of the classic French/Spanish garlic sauce – aioli – and serve it with a selection of attractively prepared vegetables and breads.

SERVES 4–6
4 garlic cloves
2 egg yolks
2.5 ml/½ tsp salt
ground black pepper
300 ml/½ pint/1¼ cups extra virgin
   olive oil
TO SERVE
red or yellow pepper, cut in thick strips
fennel, cut in slivers
radishes, halved if large
button mushrooms
broccoli florets
grissini sticks
French bread, thinly sliced

1 Crush the garlic into a bowl then beat in the egg yolks, salt and some ground black pepper.

2 Stand the bowl on a damp cloth and slowly trickle in the oil, drip by drip, whisking with a balloon whisk until you have a thick, creamy sauce. As the sauce thickens, you can add the oil in slightly larger amounts.

3 Spoon the aioli into a bowl. Arrange the dipping food around the bowl and serve lightly chilled.

Camembert Fritters

A popular starter or savoury course at the end of a leisurely dinner. These deep-fried cheeses are quite simple to do. They are served with a red onion marmalade which can be made in advance and stored in the refrigerator.

SERVES 4
MARMALADE
1 kg/2 lb red onions, sliced
45 ml/3 tbsp sunflower oil
45 ml/3 tbsp olive oil
15 ml/1 tbsp coriander berries, crushed
2 large bay leaves
45 ml/3 tbsp granulated sugar
90 ml/6 tbsp red wine vinegar
10 ml/2 tsp salt
CHEESE
8 individual portions of Camembert
1 egg, beaten
125 g/4 oz/1 cup natural colour dried
   breadcrumbs, to coat
oil, for deep fat frying

1 Make the marmalade first. In a large saucepan, gently fry the onions in the oil, covered, for 20 minutes or so or until they are soft.

2 Add the remaining marmalade ingredients, stir well and cook uncovered for a further 10–15 minutes until most of the liquid has been absorbed. Cool and then set aside.

VARIATION

You could make these fritters with fingers of firm Brie, or try it using baby goats' cheese.

3 Prepare the cheese by first scratching the mould rind lightly with a fork. Dip first in egg then in breadcrumbs to coat well. Dip and coat a second time if necessary. Store on a plate.

4 Pour oil into a deep fat fryer so it is one-third full; heat to 190°C/375°F.

5 Carefully lower the coated cheeses into the hot oil three or four at a time and fry until golden and crisp, about 2 minutes or less.

6 Drain well on kitchen paper and fry the rest, reheating the oil in between. Serve hot with some of the marmalade.

Tabbouleh 🌿

Almost the ultimate quick grain salad that simply needs soaking, draining and mixing. Bulgur is par-boiled wheat. Make this a day ahead, if possible, so that the flavours have time to develop.

SERVES 4
115 g/4 oz/¾ cup bulgur wheat
90 ml/6 tbsp fresh lemon juice
75 ml/5 tbsp extra virgin olive oil
90 ml/6 tbsp fresh parsley, chopped
60 ml/4 tbsp fresh mint, chopped
3 spring onions, finely chopped
4 firm tomatoes, skinned and chopped
salt and ground black pepper

1 Cover the bulgur with cold water and soak for 20 minutes, then drain well and squeeze out even more water from it with your hands.

2 Put the bulgur into another bowl and add all the other ingredients, stirring and seasoning well.

3 Cover and chill for a few hours, overnight, if possible.

Crudités with Houmous 🌿

Always a great family favourite, homemade houmous is speedily made with the help of a blender. The tahini paste is the secret of houmous and it is readily available in delicatessens or larger supermarkets.

SERVES 2–3
1 × 425 g/15 oz can chick peas, drained
30 ml/2 tbsp tahini paste
30 ml/2 tbsp fresh lemon juice
1 garlic clove, crushed
salt and ground black pepper
olive oil and paprika pepper, to garnish
TO SERVE
Selection of salad vegetables, e.g. cucumber, chicory, baby carrots, pepper strips, radishes
Bite size chunks of bread, e.g. pitta, walnut, naan, bruscheta, or grissini sticks

1 Put the chick peas, tahini paste, lemon juice, garlic and plenty of seasoning into a food processor or blender and mix to a smooth paste.

2 Spoon the houmous into a bowl and swirl the top with the back of a spoon. Trickle over a little olive oil and sprinkle with paprika.

3 Prepare a selection of fresh salad vegetables and chunks of your favourite fresh bread or grissini sticks into finger size pieces.

4 Set out in a colourful jumble on a large plate with the bowl of houmous in the centre. Then dip and eat!

Index